10 Winning Strategies for Leaders in the Classroom

10 Winning Strategies for Leaders in the Classroom

A Transformational Approach

Bramwell Osula   •   Renae Ideboen

$SAGE www.sagepublications.com
Los Angeles • London • New Delhi • Singapore • Washington DC

First published in 2010 by

SAGE Publications India Pvt Ltd
B1/I-1 Mohan Cooperative Industrial Area
Mathura Road, New Delhi 110 044, India
www.sagepub.in

SAGE Publications Inc
2455 Teller Road
Thousand Oaks, California 91320, USA

SAGE Publications Ltd
1 Oliver's Yard, 55 City Road
London EC1Y 1SP, United Kingdom

SAGE Publications Asia-Pacific Pte Ltd
33 Pekin Street
#02-01 Far East Square
Singapore 048763

Published by Vivek Mehra for Sage Publications India Pvt Ltd, Typeset in 11/14 Adobe Caslon Pro by Tantla Composition Pvt Ltd, Chandigarh and printed at Chaman Enterprises, New Delhi.

Library of Congress Cataloging-in-Publication Data Available

ISBN: 978-81-321-0564-0 (PB)

The SAGE Team: Rekha Natarajan, Swati Sengupta and Deepti Saxena

Dedicated to inspirational classroom leaders everywhere.

Bramwell Osula

I dedicate this book to my husband John, and daughters Alyssa and Hanna.
They are my constant joy and inspiration.

Renae Ideboen

Contents

List of Tables

List of Figures

Acknowledgments

THIS BOOK WOULD not have been possible without the patience, dedication, and support of family members, friends, colleagues, and associates. To name each of these would be a monumental task, and some would be inevitably left out. None of these people are responsible for the ideas expressed in this book or any errors that may be found. These remain entirely with the authors.

1

Leaning Forward!

THE MOST POWERFUL SPACE ON EARTH

What would you say if I told you the classroom was the most powerful space on earth? You'd probably laugh, or shake your head and point instead to a parliament building, presidential palace, the Taj Mahal, New York's Metropolitan Museum, or the Sydney Opera House. Or maybe you would reflect on the natural wonders of the world—awe-inspiring wonders like the pyramids at Giza, Roman Coliscum, Victoria Falls in Zambia, or the abundance of mystical or sacred spaces found at Britain's Stonehenge, Machu Picchu in Peru or the Ganges in India. If these are not enough, what of the canopy we call the sky and the great unknown galaxies that lie beyond what we can't see with our naked eye? Surely these are the most powerful spaces.

If we were thinking in terms of tourism, geography, or history the answer might be yes. Yet, as powerful as each of these spaces undoubtedly is, none can rival the power of the classroom to influence a community, national populace, and civilization. It doesn't matter whether the school is a one-room primitive village affair or a well-funded city institution with modern classrooms equipped with WiFi technology. Whether large or small, rich or poor, schools have the power to transform culture, deepen citizen awareness, and cultivate skills and knowledge. These are powerful, even revolutionary, objectives. Schools that respond to the challenge have the capacity to redirect the course of human history through their ability to shape minds and influence actions of students that pass through their doors.

The very first classrooms were outdoors. Parents were the natural teachers, lessons were homespun, and learning was linked to life. That was all before the tidal wave of civilization drove us all indoors, into purpose-built school buildings, and into the arms of professional teachers. Today, in classrooms all around the globe, no one has time to pause for breath. Whether in New Delhi or New York, teachers and students alike are too busy. The clock urges everyone forward, forcing us to measure progress in one second increments. In all but a few schools the clanging bell has been forgotten. This acoustic reminder of another, stricter regime when punctuality was a core requirement and school disciplinary codes were more strictly enforced has in many, especially modern schools, been replaced by a buzzer, electronic signal, or even music. To the sound of the bell, buzzer, or music students hurry from one class to the next, clutching books, chasing friends, or wrapped up in their individual thoughts.

It isn't easy being a student these days. Not that it ever was. But today seems especially challenging. There are the usual problems of preparing for exams, avoiding strict teachers, making sense of changing timetables, and fees. Even supposedly free education comes at a cost, especially if your parents are poor, live in the village, or believe that long hours spent in the classroom interfere with the performance of domestic chores. To these problems we can add the problems of career anxiety, technological change, an increasingly globalized economy—the world is shrinking—extra-curricular activities, increasing competition, and government regulations. Today, school life is much more complex than it has ever been. Our grandparents, assuming they were fortunate enough to go to school, would have difficulty recognizing modern schools for the humble and relatively simple institutions that they attended. And that's precisely the point. Today's schools are different, more complex, uncertain places.

What will tomorrow bring? Who knows? Given the current state of the world—tribal conflicts, tales of corruption, global security concerns, a deepening economic crises, voter apathy, and continuing poverty in many places—does anyone really want to know? The romantic image of the outdoor classroom where children communed with nature while learning to do simple arithmetic and write their name in uneven letters remains strangely attractive until the rain begins to fall and slowly washes away the myth. What can we do to recreate the schools of our dreams? What can we do to build the schools that students crave and society desperately needs?

Next to the home or the family, the classroom is the most powerful space on earth. Fantastic things can happen here; so can some terrible things. It all depends on our commitment. What do we intend to do with our classroom spaces? The question is not as simple as it sounds. Believe it or not, different people have different ideas concerning what the purpose of the school should be and therefore what its primary task should be. These different ideas influence the uses to which the school will be put. Do we want basic or specialized education? Should there be focus on the three R's or on "magnet schools" specializing in science, language, technology, and "global education?" Where do career preparation, education for citizenship, religion, ethics, and critical thinking enter the mix? Should schools be funded publically or privately? If the latter, should they be secular or parochial; open to all or restricted to a privileged few; or mixed or exclusive?

From the very first time schools were established, we have been asking these questions. Why not just have a mix based on national or global needs? Education policies reflect different political, economic, and religious agendas. While municipal authorities, national governments, ministers of education, and ordinary citizens consider the options, students wonder at the outcome of these debates concerning the use of their school space. At the end, it always comes down to a question of value or importance.

What value do we see in school spaces? How much importance do we really attach to the school? Assuming we can even agree as to what should take place there—the final form of the educational program or agenda—the question still remains of how we plan to manage the space. What will be the role of the principals, teachers, administrators, and oversight boards? Every generation comes bearing its hopes for a renewed classroom. Success stories are immediately seized upon. Gifted teachers, gifted students, novel teaching methods, cultural exchange programs, monetary rewards, new uniform designs, sponsorship, school meals, peer counseling, problem-based learning; the variations are almost endless. Designing a winning strategy for what is perhaps the most underrated space in most countries begins with an urgent sense of what is at stake. Considering the level of illiteracy, ignorance, and lack of preparation for the workforce that is still a problem in many countries, the classroom is an incredible center of opportunity. It isn't an exaggeration to say that the future of civilization as we know it can be won or lost here. Everything we value, whether materially or spiritually, is somehow bound up with what we do or fail to do in our classrooms.

"You can't teach me anything, so don't even try." If you've been in a classroom then you've probably encountered this attitude. Perhaps you were the one making this statement. You dared your teacher, the school, and the system to educate you. And just to prove your point you dug your heels in and clung to your defiant ways until the end of the school year or till graduation time came. Then you stood in the hallway and bragged about how badly you'd done academically or counted your write-ups or suspensions as if they were medals or smiley face stickers.

"Who cares?"

We should all care. Lucky for us not all students are defiant. Not all of them boast about tuning out. Some are hopeful and diligently plot a course to responsible citizenship. All is far from lost. However, something is missing. For every tale of success there are a dozen more stories of pain, anguish, illiteracy, and indiscipline. Classrooms are filled with students who seem to be walking through life blindly, lost in space, burned out, without hope, purpose, or a clear idea of what to do with their classroom time. What is frightening is that sometimes teachers are the ones who feel lost or burned out. Where are our leaders in the classroom?

HARD WORK AND BUCKETS OF FAITH

Long ago when men ventured out into deep waters in nothing more than paddle boats or canoes fashioned from felled trees, their families would wait patiently for them to return. No one had to say it, but a good day's fishing wasn't measured by the size of the catch. It was the safe return of the boat with all its crew that was the prayer on everyone's lips. Long before life vests and the coast guard became the norm the island's native inhabitants relied on a respect for the sea, faith in their compatriots, and common sense. These were the values that counted: respect, faith, and common sense. The only life vest on those early fishing missions was courage and the ability to swim. Treacherous waters, overhanging branches, swift currents, submerged rocks, and fate called for the best yet simplest preparation. In such cases and in a moment it could literally become a case of sink or swim. The swimmers at least had a chance. And yet men drowned, the victims of unsteady legs, larger than expected fishes, leaking vessels, bad weather, carelessness, or fate. The power of one against the raging sea may seem hopelessly one-sided. No one told the fishermen that. And they wouldn't have listened. The waters and the fish beckoned. They were fishermen. This was their life and so they smiled, gathered up the tools of their trade, and went to do what only they could do.

Transformation is alien to the classroom. Four letter syllables rarely make it into school. Even the word graduation can't always be taken for granted. Who needs a longer word when a shorter one will do? Isn't transformation just a fancy word for change? Moths become butterflies, ugly ducklings become swans, frogs become handsome princes, and barren fields yield their harvest after the rains. Transformation is remarkable change. It is the magic we seek in life. The main difference is that this remarkable change can be explained. It's nothing new. Here and there souls have always been touched, making the unremarkable remarkable.

Why should the classroom be immune to this sort of change? This is the question behind our purpose, which is to call forth transformational leaders who can bring remarkable results in the form of healing, hope, and unparalleled success to the classroom. Located somewhere within the walls of every classroom is the capacity for inspiration and positive, even startling results. Our mission is to help unlock this capacity and create a sparkle of confidence in teachers and students alike.

You'll hear it repeated over and over again that transformation takes work, hard work and bucket loads of faith. Think of it as a journey, a push and pull journey. The push is toward the largely material goals that society says we must seek. The pull on the other hand is always toward something greater than us. Trying to balance these two aspects of life is what keeps many of us awake at nights. Sometimes the tug of war we experience in our hearts is the tension between our individual goals and the call to the greatness beyond ourselves. The classroom isn't immune from the struggle. Why should it be? After all, transformation isn't promised.

The children run bare-feet to school, balancing their crudely fashioned metal "book bags" on their heads. The light ramshackle boxes contain their lesson books. Older children guide younger ones by the hand. School is a windowless building. The classroom has more in common with a cattle shed. The walls are only about three feet high, leaving a gap that extends all the way to the corrugated iron roof, which completes the rough structure. All of the children can see over the wall to the streets beyond. There are more children than schools or teachers, which means that classes are run in two shifts; one in the morning and another in the afternoon. If the principal had his way he'd introduce a third, evening shift. Transformation isn't one of the words that the teacher writes on the black board. They lean forward. The teacher is making an important point about clean hands. They pay close attention. At this rural primary school, even the six-year olds understand the value of education. During monsoon heavy rains flood the roads, concealing potholes and gutters. Undeterred, the children never miss a day. Some fashion rain caps out of plastic bags, which they wear on their heads, advertising everything from electronics and detergent to pharmaceuticals. Less daring pupils, seek temporary shelter under fruit trees or at the stalls of roadside food sellers. A few brave souls use their bags as umbrellas and continue through the deluge to school. When they arrive, everyone spends the first period after assembly baling out water. A few minutes into the baling, someone notices that the water level hasn't dropped. The classroom floor looks like a shallow somewhat muddy river. Education can't wait. The teacher, his pants rolled up unevenly, sits down and opens his book. The day's lessons begin.

Baling water probably isn't your idea of how to spend the first period of the teaching day. Your students might have something to say too. However, who is placing rocks in the river that can redirect the course of the river, and possibly alter the course of history?

As a result of increasing globalization, almost everyone is aware of what is happening elsewhere on earth. Cultural exchange programs means that even classrooms share information, although there are few exchange students in our windowless rural classroom. Leaders call for action. We must do something now. Now becomes later and today folds into tomorrow. Shifting agendas mean shifted priorities and the opportunities for transformational leadership are lost. Freedom doesn't come easily. History has shown this, time and time again. The world is crying out for leaders who understand this. Building transformational classrooms is a hard slog. Push and pull come at a price. While the coward hides behind a rock, mutters a few well-meaning words then immediately resorts to shooting arrows of doubt, true leaders build ramparts of hope and confidence. Some use bricks and mortar, commissioning new schools equipped with state-of-the-art gyms and latest computer technology. Others concentrate on innovative lesson plans and creative curriculum.

Each of these developments has its uses. They help the movement for reform. However, on their own they can't accomplish the much needed transformation. Something is missing. Unless we set the right standards, we will never be able to redirect the course of the river. Standards aren't anything new. We've been talking about standards from the very day education was institutionalized in our society. Standards of one sort or another are mandated in most school districts. While educators wrestle with implementation of standards, parents are confused by the language, and students are converted into statistics and evaluation reports. What we mean when we say that transformational classrooms need standards is that values have to be a part of any transformational plan.

What values do we want to see in our classrooms? When was the last time you had a discussion about values? What values could help you defuse the tension and decipher the often mixed messages that you receive in the classroom? What values do you desperately need to redirect the course of your classroom?

COMPASS POINTS

The invention of the compass revolutionized life for travelers. This device, said to have been invented by the Chinese thousands of years ago, literally changed the face of the world. With the compass sailors could navigate more accurately and explorers dared to cross strange oceans in search of new lands.

True leaders take charge because they know where they're going. A crisis or emergency is sometimes all it takes. Leaders do more than sit around strategizing or pointing to a need.

They do something. If only it were that easy. Leadership in the classroom or anywhere else for that matter is a slow and painful journey that will occasionally lead you through hazardous territory. Which way is forward? A thousand competing gurus and leadership experts offer their advice, pointing first this way then that. Whom should you follow? You grow dizzy. Everything in the classroom becomes a blur of faces. Somewhere in the distance you can hear clanging bells. Your confidence is sinking fast. The clanging bells are getting louder. You left your headache tablets at home. Right now the classroom is the last place you want to be.

Successful leading begins with a sense of purpose. The challenge isn't the bells that are clanging in your head. The dizziness comes and goes. Confidence doesn't matter any longer. You've abandoned all hopes of separating the blur of faces before you into distinct personalities with names. How do you embrace the change that you were seeking only yesterday? Someone is calling your name. You hear them through the clanging bells and dizziness.

"Are you okay, Mr Sen?"

The question is all it takes. As suddenly as it left you regain your sanity. You're back in charge. Mercifully, the bells have stopped. You regain your composure. This isn't your first lapse. What is this private struggle that always sets the alarm bells ringing in your head?

Don't settle into a comfortable groove or allow yourself to be carried along by the current of events. Your struggle is actually part of the process. Your desire to commit heightens the tension. Push and pull appear to be in conflict. You must ride out the storm. Begin by taking stock. Renew your commitment. Where is your classroom headed? Where are you required to lead it? Where are you now? Take a reading. Establish a baseline of values for this is the first step to redirecting the course of your classroom journey. Values matter. Without them all your commitments are hollow and the spark you hope to ignite in your classroom will never become a sparkle. At the center of the value system you want to establish is you. It makes perfect sense. Unless you are in it, it cannot be yours.

Students are capable of seeing through teachers who are unsure of themselves. Classrooms with uncertain teachers are lost classrooms. You might as well surrender your leadership at the door. In defining yourself think beyond your parents, place of birth, street address, or professional qualifications. Even the identity you sometimes wear like a name badge on your T-shirt or baseball cap isn't relevant. Think of the things that actually shape who you are. Search deep within yourself. Draw up a list of things that are really important to you. List your habits, beliefs, ideals, key principles, which if they were taken away would leave you not only naked, but totally lost. If you believe you're part of something worthwhile in life, can you define that "something?" This characterization of the real you, stripped to its bare bones, is where you begin to locate your compass points. It can be a scary place. Life is so superficial that seldom do we come face-to-face with who we really are.

Apart from the encounters in the mirror every morning as we brush our teeth or stare bleary eyed at our images, the self can be a foreigner. True compass points emerge only after we have discovered our true selves. Until then, all we can do is borrow from someone else's system of values. However, these values are not ours—they're strange. We feel uncomfortable, unsure of ourselves, the dizziness threatens a return. With the compass you can navigate more accurately and cross the strange ocean of transformational learning. As a transformational leader you must settle your values. Rebuilding the classroom is something that must be done with purpose.

Values are the habits, attitudes, influences, and commitments that keep us centered or focused. They are the touchstone of life and give it purpose. To live without values is to live a miserable and dangerous life. Miserable because values bring a refinement and noble purpose to living while the idea of an existence without some guiding system of values can leave us exposed to our base instincts. Fearing nothing, we care about nothing. The moderating forces of values challenge the tyrant that would otherwise be let loose on the world. If the world seems like a dangerous place, could a shortage of values be the problem? Think about this in relation to your classroom.

What values do you bring to the table? What influences motivate you? What values do your students bring? Have you ever thought that they might have values of their own? Values shape and define life, steering it forward. When asked if you know where you're going, having a set of values allows you to respond with a resounding, "Yes!" Schools should be wary of individuals who arrive with no clear sense of who they are or their value system. A personal statement of your philosophy of life goes some way toward filling the value gap. However, it isn't enough. The compass is a clear and detailed declaration of your personal value system. What do you stand for? What do you believe in? What are the things important to you? What motivates you or bring out the best in you? The best leaders understand who they are. Developing a set of compass points gives you a fix on your identity as a leader.

In our society, hypocrisy has become a popular mindset. Saying one thing while doing another is hypocritical. We resent our leaders when they are caught in a lie and in our own lives value the importance of consistency. Setting the right example for our children means we shouldn't tell them that it is wrong to lie, cheat, or steal, then turn around and do these things ourselves. Our values should be in alignment with who we really are. Our lives should be transparent. Living out the true purpose of one's identity with a consistent set of values makes for a more contented life. The classroom becomes a meaningful, purposeful place. From settled convictions come inspired actions. Why should the classroom be any different?

Up to now we have spoken of transformation, as if it was all about you. It isn't. Leadership is a relationship. Leaders need followers. It's a reciprocal relationship. Each feeds off the other. What leaders do is seldom their private business. The values you craft supposedly for yourself impact others. Every parent knows this. Children see and do. The environments we create at home based on our values system are an important part of the socialization process. This is what we call influence. It is also a responsibility. Our values and lives are always on display. Understanding the True North of one's moral compass has implications beyond one's immediate circle. Unless you are a hermit or castaway on a deserted island, your values affect others. The greater the size of your following the greater is your responsibility. This is why we rightly demand that our politicians, entertainers, and film stars set the right example. Teachers have a following too. In the sixties movie, *To Sir With Love*, the character played by Sydney Poitier is able to reach out to the pupils in his class by modeling the right behavior. Ignored at first, then challenged by individual students who see him as a threat, Poitier sticks to his principles, eventually winning over his students. Poitier saw his students as part of his own transformational journey. He dared to make a difference in his students' lives. So should you.

But it isn't enough just to be bold. Recklessness and folly are the dark side of daring and can ruin a classroom. Cultivating a system of values that will positively alter the flow of your classroom is a life-long journey. So, as long as you're a teacher, and even after you leave the classroom, the process of renewal continues. You check for flaws, evaluating where you might be wrong. You seek support from others, and challenge the dangers of arrogance by re-establishing your core values. The problem with so much of the discussion about values in our society is that they seldom rise above abstract statements. No wonder our students give us blank stares. While we hitch our leadership carriage to the stars, the statements we come up with must be practical. Bringing values down to earth is hard for most. We discuss the practicality of values in a later chapter. Understanding that everyone, including the most rational, cynical, or dispirited need values in order to navigate their way through life reminds us just how important compass points are. It is impossible to live a meaningful life without a set of cardinal values. Transformational classrooms are built on these values and bring purpose to leading in the classroom. Finding ones purpose restores hope to what up until now might have been seen as a hopeless journey.

CULTIVATING HOPE

"Hold onto the side, that's right, hold on tight. Now move your legs like flippers. No, don't splash. And move gently!" Mrs Simonetti, the swimming coach, had been teaching beginners how to swim for most of her 27 years as a teacher. Jessica gripped the side of the pool as Mrs Simonetti instructed and made a great show of moving her legs. She wasn't really sure how flippers moved and didn't know how much longer she could keep this up. Swimming seemed to require muscles that didn't exist. The chlorine in the water only added to her frustration. She was sure she'd go blind. Learning to swim was impossible.

"That's better. Try to keep your head up. See I told you'd get it!" Despite trying hard to concentrate and not wanting to swallow any more of the horrible water, Jessica smiled. "Close your mouth and concentrate!" Her legs were working in rhythm now. She knew it because there was less splashing and her feet weren't meeting quite as much resistance as before. The tenseness that had made her shoulders numb and the pain from unknown muscles in her thighs, legs, and feet eased. "Yes! We'll make you a pro yet!" Jessica might as well have been swimming in the Olympics. That's how proud Mrs Simonetti's comment made her feel. Maybe she'd stick with swimming after all.

Values move you to a place of hope. Let's call it the "hope zone." This is where your desire to influence others for good is revived. Hope challenges the lethargy brought on by years of non-transformational teaching and the abandonment of clear principles. Hope prepares you for the journey and will make all the difference in what will become the transformational journey of a lifetime.

Transformational teachers like Mrs Simonetti are hopeful. Their classrooms, even if it is a swimming pool, reflect this hope. So do their students. Hope isn't the same as happiness, although one is more likely to produce the second. Classrooms without hope are bleak; unpromising places where students and teachers alike are resigned to failure. The unfortunate thing about our society is that classrooms like this exist. Working to reverse this tide and to restore hope is a burden of transformational teaching. Teachers are witnesses to heartbreak and misfortune every day. These illustrate society's hopelessness. Various forms of counseling reflect some of society's social pathologies. Between the psychologists, sociologists, and social workers is the teacher who must deal with the malfunction. Inspiration is still one of the best antidotes for misery. However, inspiration is predicated on hope.

Hope has a wide currency, which even the die-hard despondent finds difficult to reject. If there is one thing that connects all human beings, it is the desire for hope. Hope more than happiness or even peace is the real story of humanity. Of all winning strategies for classroom leaders any which are aimed at increasing hope are priceless. The real definition of a tyrant is one who denies or withholds hope. Transformational teachers have to defeat the tyrant in the classroom. One way of doing this is to recreate the classroom as a place where hope can flourish. In some communities, peace gardens or parks have become quite popular. Why shouldn't hope zones? Why should we rely on motivational speakers who are parachuted in to dispense their canned hope only to withdraw and return again the following year?

The hope zone isn't a physical place like the peace gardens in some communities, where teachers and students go to meditate or to escape from the press of the classroom. Rest and renewal are important. Guidance counselors and gurus can make a difference. Hope is the stock in trade of social workers and spiritual advisors. For the teacher, hope begins as a positive attitude of mind but extends to every part of one's being. Hope is infectious. It radiates outwards from the core of an individual stirring up others and defying the bleak spirits. The hope zone is where we work out the ragged pieces of our existence. The result is a belief in the potential for good. Apathy and cynicism are chased away and replaced with a grounded optimism.

Whether you are male or female, students should have no problem seeing you as a source of hope. Hope is grounded in what they see as your core values, what we call your compass points. The two go together. When you recognize the limitless possibilities of your classroom you connect with the fire inside of you.

When you enter the hope zone you declare who you are. Hope says you are committed to and passionate about your vocation. You understand the meaning of the word "vocation" and what you have been called to do. You don't know everything—who does? Hope keeps you expectant, ready, willing, and leaning forward. You find a good reason to remain where you are. The answers to the questions that still remain will come. You exercise patience but search for the answers daily spurred on by your belief in the power of the transformational classroom.

Success—the success of your students—was high on your list of reasons for deciding to become a teacher. You wanted your students to succeed; to inspire them to be the best of their generation. This was your reason for entering the classroom. The search for success is almost as powerful as the quest for hope. Everyone wants to succeed and you are no different. However, your skills and talents seem inadequate for the task. At the end of each day you are physically and emotionally exhausted. Yet you go on.

The details of your personal agenda for change haven't been worked out yet. Somewhere deep in your heart something is being rekindled. You aren't sure what to call it. You are sure it isn't the daily administrative rituals or even the paycheck that keep you coming back to the classroom. Something inside of you refuses to let go. Each night you dream of finding the transformational path in your classroom. You pray that the classroom demons will leave you alone. While you churn inside, frustrated, bitter, and perhaps even angry, the yearning remains. This yearning is the hope. Capturing the hope will liberate your spirit and set you on the road to being a visionary in the classroom. Finally, your professional and personal values are connected.

Today, there is an urgency for teachers to collectively identify their hope in the future of the classroom. Dialogue is important. You have to share and speak with others. None of us can succeed alone. As a leader you must communicate your personal values. This is an indispensable part of developing others. Communicating hope is the springboard to lasting change in the classroom. What you envision for yourself is what you will communicate to others. Your students profit from the lessons that you share. Hope says: We can do this. Together, success is possible. The classroom becomes a place where good things can happen.

CONNECTING THE HEAD AND THE HEART (THE TRANSFORMATIONAL MANDATE)

Your call is to be the best leader that you can be in the classroom. To achieve this you must connect your head and your heart, commit to a program of change, and review this program at regular intervals. The transformational mandate is the call to move from professional duty or contractual obligation to empowering others. Students should be made more aware of their own transformational abilities. The quality of the transformation will depend on your level of commitment. This is manifested in your values. Commitment and values go together. The transformational objective demands that you find the seemingly elusive *summum bonum* or highest good. In advertising terms, the *summum bonum* is your brand value. Have you figured out your brand value? Is it obvious every time you walk into the classroom?

In the commercial world different brands compete for a share of the market. Asserting your transformational brand can be difficult in the classroom where many different voices vie for recognition. However, leadership isn't a competition to see who can shout the loudest. If it was, you would probably lose. Neither is it a race to see who can get to the finish line first. Transformational leaders guide others past their own resistance with courage, humility, and understanding. This is the real test of leadership; to serve in the face of opposition. Transformational leaders serve even, or especially, in situations where others resist. This is one of the hallmarks of great classroom leadership: to serve in the face of opposition. Classrooms are a great place to cultivate the qualities of transformational leadership.

In order to be a transformational classroom leader you must recapture the vocational spirit. Transformational teaching addresses the urgency of building moral virtues into the classroom from the inside out. It connects your head with your heart and produces courage of purpose. When students are shown the path toward safety and security they develop trust. Pursuing excellence in an environment of trust and with a boundless sense of hope is the crying need of your classroom. Trust makes it possible to remodel your classroom; one individual student at a time. It's hard to ignore the thought that commitment to others and cooperation seem to go against the grain in our present culture. Pushing past the barrier of self-centeredness will uncover your maturity as a transformational teacher.

CROSSING BORDERS

Values have undergone a profound change in our society. The rate and pace of this change has been greatest in the last 50 years. In some ways popular culture has taken over as a major leadership influence. A revival of values in the classroom is one way of equipping future generations with the moral tools needed to handle the fallout of popular culture. But values aren't just a preoccupation of leaders in the so-called developed nations of the world. In places as diverse as India, Brazil, South Africa, and Israel leaders and ordinary citizens are struggling with similar questions of values. In fact, it's a universal struggle. No one is immune.

The banner headlines point to escalating violence, ethnic conflicts, AIDS, poverty, global warming, genocide, nuclear weapons, biodiversity, and terrorism. Now, more than at any other time in the world's history, we are all connected. Values affect us all. Every major institution in society, whether it is the family, the government, business, the military, or education is affected. Values reach into every corner of the globe shaping everything we do. On the global stage, leaders talk about the importance of standing up and being counted. We judge them for their embrace of specific values—questions of character—as much as for their performance.

Successful leaders are the ones whose leadership appears to be guided by a clear moral compass. What takes place on the global stage is reflected in the classroom. Teachers must demonstrate courage and sign up to a value-based learning agenda. New forms of intellectual, emotional, and spiritual intelligence are an important part of this new agenda. The clear message is that none of us can sit back and expect change to happen on its own. Being passive is not a viable option. Classroom leaders have to be active. Living in the transformational space that you help to create, buoyed up by a deep passion to help your students succeed in a competitive global environment, makes you both confident and humble about the capacity for change. You embrace the seemingly endless array of possibilities and encourage those in your charge to believe in something greater than themselves.

As we think about what is happening globally we see the need to cross borders. In the same way that classrooms everywhere are connected through education and learning, values also reach beyond the local classroom. What is the global or universal reach of your values? Where do your values connect or collide with others? Should core values be limited or defined by culture and location? How will you teach values within the context of diversity? What is the real value of your highest ideals if they do not take you and your students beyond the immediate cultural environment? This book offer possible answers to this practical question.

SUCCEEDING

To succeed in the classroom you need a plan framed in commitment. To reach your destination you must feel a real sense of purpose and progress. You can't afford to be moderate about your transformational commitment. The mission must define who you are. Because it defines you, it transforms others in the classroom. The values that you espouse must be real. The condition of your classroom demands your attention. You're in charge. You're also in the firing line. Accountability and responsibility go together. You need strategies and tools that will work in your particular situation.

Teachers are society's frontline practitioners. They are the ones who lead the reforms in the classroom. The public and the government have an obvious investment in the process. Together, all can benefit from what conscientious leaders accomplish in the classroom. Civilization turns, slowly or swiftly, on the quality of its teachers and the quality of the students produced by our schools.

Developing winning strategies for the classroom identifies the transformational possibilities that lie within our grasp. Winners in the classroom interpret life as an unfolding, hope-filled prospect. Making a commitment to good teaching may seem much too simple a proposition. Some of the best discoveries in life are also the simplest. Stripped to its core, the message of transformation is remarkably simple. Values and hope create a powerful force that will liberate classrooms as well as communities. The benefits of transformational classroom leadership ripple outward.

2

True Grit

The Courage to Get It Right

Never underestimate your power to change yourself.
Never underestimate your power to change others.

~Viktor Frankl

STRATEGY: DEVELOP YOUR VALUE SYSTEM

VALUES LEAD

A few weeks into the new semester of a high school ethics class, the students were asked to make a list of their top 10 values. Almost everyone stared into space for a while. A few students slowly started to write a few things down. One student raised his hand. "What do you mean by values?" he asked.

The question is an appropriate one and one that has a history of relevance to the human race. What is embraced as a value covers a broad spectrum. It is what we value that determines our course of action. So, values have deep meaning in that they send us on specific journeys.

Values serve a useful purpose. They help us make sense of the world around us. In a nutshell, a value is something that we cherish. They are our core principles. It is what we find in life that has merit. It is what we respect and believe has significance. Our values shape the way we view the world. There are a lot of factors that play into our worldview. Where we grow up, our family ties, our spiritual development, and our economic status—all play a part in our perceptions. It is our perceptions that drive what we eventually accept and cherish and what we reject (Nash, 1992:16). This is important because we may think that we are at the mercy of the circumstances that we find ourselves in. The opposite holds true. Our values aid us in shaping circumstances. Our values add meaning to the events of our lives and we can learn and grow from them.

In essence, values shape character. Character influences our decision-making processes. It is easy to see if a person embraces strong purposeful values by the way they act. You may have heard the expression, "actions speak louder than words." This is true. Actions are a result of the values that we embrace. When facing difficulties, a strong value system will strengthen character. On the other hand, a weak value system can make trials seem more chaotic because it is hard to find balance when you are not sure about what you believe and can hold on to. Lack of balance can cause you to mistrust your own decisions. It can also cause others to doubt your abilities on many levels. As a leader it is vital that others see you as trustworthy. To be trustworthy is to demonstrate strong character based on sound values.

At this time, you may find it difficult to express specifics about your worldview and you may find it even more difficult to break it down into a list of specific values. It is important to recognize what you cherish deeply and analyze the meaning it has in shaping you and others around you. As you discover your values and explore their depth you will also notice an emerging purpose in life. Your values will establish whether you have credibility as a leader. Your values will shape the way you understand your life's work. They shape the way you treat yourself and those around you.

With values taking such an important role in thinking and the resulting actions, it would seem to make sense to pay close attention to our values. Accepting and rejecting values helps us define our destination. If you examine your life and believe that it is moving in the direction that pleases you, then you probably have taken the time to evaluate your values. Conversely, if you examine your course and recognize that your values are leading you on a path of destruction, then you have not intentionally developed balance. In order for your life to have meaning, you must understand that values play a powerful as well as integral part. They are functional and they help to meet specific objectives.

Imagine a young athlete that is nurtured to develop the value of healthy competition. He determines a course of fitness that will ensure him a coveted spot on his favorite team. Along the way, he makes decisions that cause him to believe that a sound mind and fit body are worth the pain and discipline needed to equip him for success. He studies the foods that will fuel him correctly. He incorporates the physical fitness required to develop his muscles. He follows a strict regimen of self control until his education, insights, and effort bring about the rewards that he desires. His values have deep meaning to him and they help him to meet his objectives.

Suppose that this athlete sets his course of action and discovers along the way that he has a physical impediment that does not allow him to complete his dream. He is told he will never again be able to compete. All of his hard work and discipline will no longer garner the results he dreamed and work so hard to achieve. You can probably imagine that this would be a crushing blow. His view of the world around him may be altered dramatically because circumstances have presented another view of what could be. He would be forced to re-examine his options and discover a new order of things. His choices from the time he discovered that his original plan changed would act as a fork in the road. If he examines the facts and embraces the shift in his course, he may be able to transform his original values into an even deeper set of values that draw more substance into his character.

There is also another possibility. If the athlete allowed the new circumstances to embitter him, he may find that his values were weak and are now acting to debilitate him. He might fret day and night about the loss of his goal and feel that the circumstances left him with little or no hope. You might hear him say, "I'm angry. This is not what I planned. I am jealous and resentful of my fellow team mates who seem to have everything going for them. All my hard work is useless."

In life there are many forks in the road. When circumstances are presented, they can either strengthen values or weaken them. Values transform your character. It is up to you to decide. It is at this very point that some people become confused and lose their way. Some take hold of what they believe has deep meaning and channel their beliefs in a new and exciting direction. When faced with challenging circumstances, some people find it difficult to move forward and fall into an inward spiral of grief and resentment. This is the point of transformation. Either way, when the fork in the road is presented, you will be transformed into a being of light or a being of darkness based on the type of values that you embrace. Since values are transformational they hold power. What we value we act upon. What we act upon determines our character. You hold the power to change your circumstances by drawing from the well of pre-determined values. As we are transformed we become the likeness of what we hold dear. If you've taken the time to know who you are and what you deeply believe in, you will be able to choose wisely when the fork in the road presents options.

The former President of the US, Ronald Reagan, saw that character is a bi-product of a value system. He said:

> The character that takes command in moments of critical choices has already been determined. It has been determined by a thousand other choices made earlier in seemingly unimportant moments. It has been determined by all those little choices of years past-by all those times when the voice of conscience was at war with the voice of temptation-whispering a lie that 'it doesn't really matter.' It has been determined by all the day-to-day decisions made when life seemed easy and crises seemed far away, the decisions that piece by piece, bit by bit, developed habits of discipline or of laziness; habits of self-sacrifice or self- indulgence; habits of duty and honor and integrity or dishonor and shame. (Ronald Regan quoted in Daft, 2002: 129)

EXCEPTIONAL VALUES LEAD TO EXCEPTIONAL CHANGE

If the values that we embrace have the power to shape our individual lives, they certainly have the power to shape others. The transformation that takes place in our own hearts as we seek to shape our value system, needs to be tended. As Ronald Reagan pointed out, your character is a choice (Daft, 2002). The choices that you make individually are ones that influence your relationships corporately.

Imagine the coach of the young athlete that we discussed earlier. The coach has a definite influence on the team. During the coach's lifetime, he made the little decisions that lead him to become a great leader. He understands, through years of careful study and attendance of specific actions that the mind of an athlete must be nurtured. He recognizes that day-to-day disciplined behavior is required. He also knows that each member of the team has profound influence on the outcome of the bigger picture—the game. During the practices the coach carefully weaves a picture into the athletes' minds of what success looks like. The image becomes stronger as each athlete embraces the small choices to balance their lives to reflect the vision that has been cast.

The coach will have influence over the team as long as the values he attempts to infuse are the values that he also embraces. To say that he believes in a balanced lifestyle and demonstrates that he cares nothing of the discipline of a balanced life, his followers will not accept his leadership. Soon, they will fall away and nothing will be gained.

If you set your goal to lead, you must plan to set your goal for understanding how your values affect your character because others too are affected by your character. Plan to assess your values carefully to line up with the actions that you take daily. Conscientious assessment of values requires an intentional process of development from the inside out.

Let's look at the idea of conscientious assessment. What is it? We will continue with the example of the coach. All coaches have one thing in common. They motivate the followers in a vision of what can be. Their aim is to help their followers flourish and grow into effective individuals that make a difference corporately. There is a correlation between self-mastery and change. People who are able to learn how to balance their thoughts and deeds are able to successfully move from inaction and apathy to action and purpose.

Coaching is a transformational process. All leaders are coaches. They help followers move in specific directions. They have values that they believe in and seek to influence others in a like-minded course of action. The coach structures the message in a way that makes sense to the team. They communicate the logical steps that must be taken to reach the type of character that proves to be worthy of a good team player. You may ask how does the coach know how to develop this character in his followers? He knows because he has taken the time to meticulously examine his own values and he recognizes that conscientious attention to detail will garner results.

Conversely, you may at one time have been a follower under a leader who lacked clear direction. Do the followers trust the leader who lacks direction and sound character? Do they rally on a path that yields positive and enriching experiences? A leader that lacks character rarely takes followers on a productive path. At some point followers recognize that poor character leads to deception and chaos. Balance in leadership can only be maintained when the leader can be trusted (Covey, 2004: 161).

The first step in balancing your own leadership is to understand that your personal choices affect everyone around you. Personal values play an important role in your decision-making process but in broader terms they have an outward manifestation that affects many for generations to come. Helping others to make sense of their lives and to follow a course of self construction rather then self destruction is a transformational process that starts with your own transformation. If your intention is to aid others in a message of hope and positive change, then your own message should be credible and trustworthy. We all are teachers. We are teaching others aspects of humanness that matter throughout the ages. A good foundation will support your own future as well as the people who follow.

In the classroom what the teacher says or does is a matter of public record. Even those things that may be said or done behind closed doors do not remain hidden for very long. This is why linking personal and social values are important. Students are constantly looking for a credibility gap in their teachers, coaches, and leaders. Values are an obvious place to find these gaps. If you want to be an effective leader then you must find the doorway that will lead from who you are to who others can be. What this tells us is that leadership is intentional. Leaders who understand their values intentionally set forth to understand the world in which they find themselves, and seek ways to make it better not simply for themselves but for others around them.

YOUR UNIQUE STORY

Earlier we defined worldview as your own unique story. Within that story you have had trials and tribulations, joys and successes, hopes fulfilled and hopes dashed. The story has shaped your perceptions and from your perceptions you have developed skills. As you begin to develop your personal value system, you should take stock of where you stand to date. In this chapter we will teach you the effective tool of Personal Analysis (PA). A PA will help you get a panoramic view of your life. As you develop the panoramic view you will begin to see how values have shaped your perceptions in the past and what you can do to help move your life forward in a meaningful direction. You will also notice that you will need to develop some new values in order to bring about positive change.

Your values are your core priorities. In a sense, they are organic in that they will change over time. Early in your life your values are shaped by your parents or people who raise you. Your teachers and friends influence your values. As you develop, you begin to see that you may have values that are distinctly different. This is part of your own story. It is unique because no one has the exact same circumstances that you have. You can develop your own life's balance by looking specifically at what holds meaning to you and what doesn't. Before you can lead others, you must be able to master your own life successfully. If you can clearly define your purpose, you can help others find theirs. Imagine the powerful impact that you have because you are unique and have a specific purpose for your existence. Grasping the importance of our individual influence on events is vital in effective leadership. It places a great deal of weight on the need for a sound value system that clearly demonstrates a direction that others can model.

CRAFTING A VALUE SYSTEM

Did you know that we often get in the way of our own improvement? One of the top reasons people struggle with making significant progress in their lives is because of procrastination.

Almost everyone struggles with procrastination, which can directly be related to fear, worry, and doubt. The tools that we are going to give you will guide you through a process of analysis that will effectively help you to gain balance with the first step. As you begin to craft your value system you will be surprised to see the unique attributes that you can build on. As you build them you will become more and more successful in your personal goals and that will ultimately affect your leadership style. Having effective tools to offer others will help them in building confidence in themselves and in your leadership. Remember that an effective leader is one that can clearly be trusted by leading the way with confidence.

Value systems that recognize purpose and a vision of a desired future, open doors to creative and hopeful thinking. Examine the following three character qualities. Imagine how improving these areas will aid you with your personal balance. Is there someone in your sphere of influence that will benefit as you develop them intentionally?

- **Confidence:** As you craft your value system you will become more confident in your ability to influence positive change. As you witness change in yourself and in your followers, you will feel successful. Your success will be based on lasting attributes such as increased ability in effective decision-making, better attitude, greater vision, and a heightened sense of motivation.
- **Emotional intelligence:** Your value statements will help you understand your emotions on a deeper level. Your values drive your actions but they also guide your reactions. Emotions such as love, anger, enjoyment, disgust, and fear will take on new meaning as you filter them through a set of workable values. For instance, imagine that you choose the value of respect. Your emotions will follow a course that upholds the value of respect. You will be more cooperative, show love, and repress anger. If you recognize, for instance, that anger is a problem, you will seek ways to bridle that emotion. As you become more successful in dealing with your emotions you become more emotionally intelligent. Emotional intelligence increases self efficacy. It also increases your people skills (Goleman, 2002).
- **Hope:** The hope zone is vital in personal, effectual growth. Hope sets goals and recognizes the value of achieving them. If you live in the hope zone you become more self-motivated because you realize that your hope has purpose. Your values will identify pathways for successful living. The more successful you become at reaching your goals, the more your hope will increase. If you live in the hope zone you won't be daunted by the fork in the road. You will see every new fork in the road as an opportunity rather than a threat or disaster.

YOU-AS-COACH

A coach is a person who analyzes resources and uses them wisely. As you move through the PA system, you will start to uncover hidden resources. Using your resources will help you become a better decision-maker. Your decisions affect the future powerfully. Just for a moment consider your ancestors. Did the people they marry and the way they lived affect you? What decisions did your ancestors make that determined where you grew up? How did their life's work affect your education? Did their decisions affect your friendships and opportunities? When you consider the lasting effect your decisions have on the future it is easy to see the importance of building values that bring about hope to you and others. A good coach knows how to maximize opportunities and eliminate threats. Let's get started!

BUILDING A PERSONAL ANALYSIS (PA) SYSTEM

A Personal Analysis (PA) is going to be your best tool in discovering a fruitful and balanced life. To begin your analysis you are going to need a few items. It is best to have a binder that can have pages added to it as your PA will be an ongoing process. Some people have added color coding and labels. You will develop your own style as you move through the process. For now, a three-ring binder with blank pages will get you started.

The first part of your PA is going to be called the SWOT. A SWOT is an analysis of your Strengths, Weaknesses, Opportunities, and Threats (Jones and George, 2003: 262). Your PA will use the SWOT format but it will lead you to make conclusions that will help you develop and shape your purpose.

Set up the following sections in your binder. You will add other sections in future chapters.

✓ STRENGTHS
✓ WEAKNESSES
✓ OPPORTUNITIES
✓ THREATS
✓ RESOURCES
✓ VALUE CONSTRUCTION
✓ ACTION STEPS

STRENGTHS

The greatest part of your PA is going to be your section on strengths. In your strength section, list everything that you can think of that makes you strong. This section can have categories such as skills, character qualities, and specific resources. You might list attributes that make you feel physically, mentally, or spiritually strong. In other words, list everything and anything that you can think of that you feel are your special gifts. To start you off we will offer some categories that will get you thinking in the right direction. You may come up with some of your own categories that make you unique. Be honest with yourself. If you are like most people, they are quick to write a long list of weaknesses but struggle to admit that they are strong. Here are some starter categories:

- Personal skills
- Education
- Unique qualities
- Talents
- Achievements

One woman shared her strength list in a seminar. It was an impressive list of attributes. It was interesting because she said that when she started making her list she couldn't think of anything that made her strong. She had recently emerged from a bitter loss in her life and had difficulty seeing her self-worth. This is the case with many people. It is for this reason that your list will be vital in your present and future growth. At a later date you will see how these areas have directly influenced circumstances and the lives of many.

Here are some entries that some seminar participants shared.

I am:

Dependable	Forgiving	Kind
Loving	Purposeful	Patient (most of the time)
Helpful	Open to education	Cooperative
Full of energy	Trusting	Courageous
Versatile	A skilled musician	Loyal
Flexible	Determined	Forward thinking
Willing	Trust-worthy	Friendly to strangers
Competent	Organized	Good with animals

Your Strength section should be a thoughtful list. Beside every entry jot down in a bullet-point fashion a note about that strength. For example:

- Dependable: My family and friends can count on me. I show up for work and contribute substantially to my employer.
- Cooperative: I don't demand my own way. I try to listen carefully and look at other points of view.
- Forward-thinking: I have a positive outlook toward emerging opportunities. I am creative and innovative in my thinking.

In order to maximize your self-efficacy look carefully at each category and add to your strength section as new ones come to mind. By adding bullet-point details you will later be able to match areas of need to your strengths. Ask friends, family, teachers, and co-workers how they view your strengths. Ask for specifics and add them to your list. A word of caution:

only add truthful strengths in this section. A long list of imaginative adjectives will not help you as a self coach. Remember that a coach looks at real strengths and resources and begins building from that point. A list of hopeful strengths will have its place in a later exercise. Right now you should concentrate on thinking about your attributes to date. This will be an ongoing list and it will be one of your most exciting sections. Be honest and thorough.

WEAKNESSES

For some people, weaknesses are hard to admit. For others weaknesses are recognized so strongly that it is difficult to overcome. This section will help to set you free of ongoing weak areas and help you to analyze effective improvement. Here are some examples to get you started.

- Avoid challenges
- Question authority
- Resist change
- Anger
- Resentment
- Fear
- Envy
- Procrastination

The key point about a weakness is that as soon as you recognize it you've taken the first step in accepting the challenge to overcome it. We call it the first step because it takes effort and planning to move forward. The power that a weakness has over an individual is that it is permitted to continue unabated. Coaches analyze weaknesses and look for viable solutions. As a self-coach taking the time to review weak areas is a positive move toward intervening to turn away from an area that is causing you to lose ground.

After taking the challenge to face weakness, Nicko, a student in Japan, wrote:

I have an anger problem. For years I blamed my parents for my anger but it suddenly occurred to me that I was the author of my own dissatisfaction. One day, I sat down and wrote a list of things that I was angry about and a surprising thing was revealed. Almost all of my anger had to do with my own inability to step forward and be responsible for my own actions. I used the past as a type of crutch so that I didn't have to make changes. I recognize that I am lazy. It is easier to blame others rather than to take responsibility for myself. After acknowledging this I did a lot of soul searching. I made another list of what I would do in the future to overcome my anger. One of my core strengths that I listed is that I am determined. I wanted to use that determination to my best advantage and determine that I will change. A year later I looked back at my original list and it was surprising to see how much I improved in a short time. I am a happier person because I took the time to face my anger and tame it. I am excited about improving other areas of my life. Someday I hope to say that I have conquered anger completely. Each time I feel this emotion I return to my note book and write down the cause for what I'm feeling and the steps I will take to defeat it. (Fictional anecdote by author).

As you write a few bullet-points in your subsection, add the date on which you recognize these areas in your life. This is important because as you move through this book you will discover ways to overcome some of the difficulties you are having that interrupts your balance. Over the course of time you will be able to conquer these areas by admitting them and moving toward solutions. It is important to date them so that when you overcome a specific area you will find a great sense of accomplishment. This is valuable because it allows you to move forward in your life instead of continually revisiting old areas of pain. Succeeding in overpowering weak areas requires attention to detail. You may feel overwhelmed by specific areas of weaknesses but you can face them with a whole new attitude of achievement by taking small and decisive action steps. Notice that we said small. Moving forward is never in leaps and bounds. Think of this. We never move forward in time by months or years. We move forward by seconds and minutes, then by hours and days. Each second is a small yet important unit in itself. Improvement is the same way. Improve in small units. Break down the change so that you only have to do one small thing at a time. Take the time to enjoy the journey.

After teaching this concept in a seminar one man asked. "How can I enjoy the journey of something that has caused me pain and misery?" The answer is simple. From this point on, you can acknowledge a weak area and make a plan to do one small thing towards change. Begin taking notes on your small victories. As you begin to move down the road toward self improvement write down the little triumphs and celebrate them. As you start to celebrate you will see that your journey is building your character. You are not helpless and you have great hope in achieving your plan. After some months have passed, you will see from your dated entries that you are very powerful. Not only did you succeed in moving forward, you have a detailed plan on how you did it. You will be inspirational in helping others to succeed. Isn't that an enjoyable journey?

Sometimes weakness, if analyzed properly, can be categorized easily into fear, procrastination, and lack of self-confidence. This is where your strength section becomes valuable. In your tool box of gifts you already have a strength that corresponds to your weakness. For instance, Nicko recognized that his strength of determination could be directly applied to solving his problem. After you've written down your weaknesses look for a strength that will aid you in building your action plan.

OPPORTUNITY

This is one of the most exciting parts of the SWOT analysis. Often people miss an opportunity because they don't recognize it. We will give you an example to iterate the point. A good friend of ours worked as a banker for over a decade in a well established bank. Her job seemed very stable and she met dozens of influential people daily. She built relationships with them but failed to see that they might be a part of her future. One day the bank announced that they were undercapitalized and would be closed. Her job was suddenly and immediately terminated. She was in shock. She wondered where she would get a job. If she had collected the business cards of the people she came in contact with daily, she would have a resource of people she could network with to help her in a job search.

Opportunities come in many forms. If you have a section of opportunities it will be at the forefront of your mind. Opportunities can slip by if we are not prepared to take advantage of them. Not every opportunity is timely. That is why you should always date your entries so that you can be sure later when the opportunity presented itself. Here are some examples of opportunities to help you think in the right direction.

Job opportunity: June 8, 2008—Met William Jones, Bank President. Mentioned to give him a call if I ever wanted to make a change. (See saved business card).

Roommate opportunity: July 5, 2009—Susan Anthony said to follow up with her in October as she will be moving into a house and will need a room mate. (Make note on calendar).

Review opportunities frequently. It will become easy to link opportunities when you have solid inventory. Some people have reported that after keeping track of specific opportunities they were able to find solutions to challenges as they arose with little effort. We all think that we will remember details but the simple truth is that we don't. Small entries in your journal may capture information that will be useful in the future.

The details in this section are exceedingly valuable. As you build your SWOT you will begin to see linkages. The links between your strengths and your opportunities will become apparent when they are written down.

Another friend had an exciting opportunity presented to her when she was asked to serve as a board member of a local college. The president handed her a sheet with the qualification requirements. One of the requirements was that every board member had to have a graduate degree. She approached the president and said that she would have to decline because she didn't meet that requirement. He thought about it a moment and then offered a reduced tuition rate if she would enroll in their school. She was thrilled. This was an opportunity that she couldn't refuse. Immediately she recognized that one of her weak areas was procrastinating finishing her degree. This opportunity allowed her to meet one of her weak areas head-on. She dated both the weak area and the opportunity area with a sub-section note that she was making progress, and finally overcame the nagging pain of putting off one of her life goals.

Later, you will see how goals line up with these sections but for now it is important to recognize an opportunity as it presents itself. This is an ongoing process. If you move through time and none of your opportunities come to pass, then you will need to examine the question of "why?". What is it about your personality that keeps you from moving forward? Is it fear? Is it procrastination? Is it lack of confidence? These are questions that will present themselves as you analyze your entries. The dates are important so that you make time-bound goals.

THREATS

Threats are the more serious side of your SWOT. Threats are what keep you awake at night worrying. They are the elements of doubt that cause you to take pause over your circumstances. While some threats can be serious, others are imagined. The point is that it doesn't matter if a threat is real or imagined, it has the same effect. Threats are crippling. They can distort your judgment. They can cause you to make rash decisions. They can cause you to lose balance. It is for these short reasons out of many that threats should be recognized so that you can find a viable solution. By placing them on paper you are allowing yourself to take hold of your situation and allow opportunities to take root. Imagine that the entry made earlier in June in your opportunity section was the meeting with William Jones, the bank president. It is now a year later and you forgot about his comments. But as you write an entry in your threat section about your impending job loss you begin to review your past year's opportunities. Suddenly you remember meeting Mr Jones and you give him a call. He welcomes your call and sets up an interview. Instead of your threat taking root and causing you to spin into fear, you quickly find a way to move your threat into becoming an opportunity.

Threats, like weaknesses can be minimized with an action plan. Look for solutions in your tool box of strengths. With bullet-point detail write down corresponding strengths and jot down small steps that you can take to regain balance. Instead of dwelling in fear and negative reactions look for answers. The key thing about threats and weaknesses is that they are related. You should, however, recognize that strength and opportunity are also related and are the counter point that offers solutions to life's struggles. This revelation will help you restore balance when circumstances cause you to falter. Many have noted that dating their entries was useful in recognizing that solutions are never far away. It is very exciting to see that often solutions are waiting in the wings if we only take inventory of the tools that we have. This is why it is essential to continue making entries in your Strengths and Opportunities sections. New tools will often help solve problems as they arise. Identification of the tools aids the process of using the right tool for the job. Does this make sense?

RESOURCES

This section is also a very valuable tool. It helps you to keep track of special resources that helped you along the way. This section is an easy reference for you when you need to solve a particular problem in the future or help others with similar challenges. Keeping track of your resources is helpful in almost every category. Your notes can be brief but detailed enough to help you quickly locate a tool when needed.

Books (fictional examples):
The Power of Forgiveness by C. Lilly. Note: Chapter 2 particularly helpful with anger management. Sept 2009.

Keep Your Distance by John Powers. Note: Whole book helped with family relationships. Aug 2008.

Seminars (fictional example):
Motivating Your Students by Alice Mills in July 2009. Great handouts on keeping students action-oriented. (See file).

Everyone thinks that they will remember when and where they were when they made a helpful discovery. The fact is, as time goes on our minds have a tendency to forget important facts that helped build our roadmap of success. Short notes will help you to see that resources are powerful tools in meeting your goals. Keep track of them.

VALUE CONSTRUCTION

Now that you've made entries in your PA with your SWOT analysis (Jones and George, 2003) it is time to take inventory of your values. As we stated earlier, if you cherish something you will take action. Values are an essential part of taking action steps to solve particular challenges in every day life. In the next section you will see how your values and your SWOT will give you the exact answers that you are looking for in building a productive and happy future. But before you get to that point it is essential to analyze what you accept and what you reject in your value system. In this section you will make lists as you did in the SWOT section with a few bullet-point entries. By writing your values down you will start to realize the power of your values in your constructive journey. This exercise is especially useful to you as a leader because it will help you to get a broad vision of your life's purpose. It is the tool that will help you teach others to build their value system. It is the answer for working out life's challenges.

Write down everything that you cherish. In the chart below there are lists of some instrumental and terminal values (Johnson, 2001: 66). They will provide a starting point. They may not list all of the things that you value. They will help you to start thinking in the right direction.

As you work through your action steps keep your value list at hand. Acting consistently with your values is a vital part of leadership. Followers need leaders to clearly know that their decisions follow suit with their stated values. Your decision-making capabilities will improve as you move through your Personal Analysis and understand the strengths that allow you to improve and change.

ACTION STEPS

SWOT Analysis

The Action Steps section is one of the most valuable parts of your personal analysis. As we stated earlier, when you are faced with a problem to solve you have a number of ways that you can approach it according to your values. The Action Step section is the place to make entries on the challenge you are facing. It will help you to take stock of your personal values, strengths and opportunities and match them against the weakness and threats that you've identified.

✓ **Step 1:** Write out the challenge. Date it.
✓ **Step 2:** Write down a corresponding strength. Date it.
✓ **Step 3:** Write down several values that will help you make a decision.
✓ **Step 4:** Check your Opportunity section for possible solutions.
✓ **Step 5:** Decide on three small action steps to take immediately. Write them down. Date them. Begin taking action.
✓ **Step 6:** Decide on three long term maintenance steps. Write them down. Date them.
✓ **Step 7:** Journal the action step progress. Watch for opportunities. Date them.
✓ **Step 8:** Celebrate successes.

Here are some examples:

Challenge: Finding a suitable roommate.

Strengths: Organized
Caring
Respectful of other's time
Personable
Truthful
Good health habits

Values: Trustworthiness
Kindness
Honesty
Independent

Opportunities: Trusted co-worker's sister looking for a roommate (3/29/09).

Immediate Action Steps:
• Begin writing down specific needs for the ideal roommate situation. Consider values and strengths.
• Follow up with co-worker from opportunity dated 3/29/09. Ask friends if they know of someone that meets my criteria for an ideal roommate.
• Post a notice of need at my volunteer organization.

Long-term Action Steps:
• Keep a journal of opportunities for future roommates.
• Maintain consistency with values in decision-making daily.
• Follow through with strengths and look for ways to overcome specific weakness.

Progress:

- July 1, 2009 Interviewed co-worker's sister. She seems like a good match but have three other possible candidates. Will decide by August 16.
- July 5, 2009 Threat: Need to raise half of the rent by July 20. Must make decision and seek funds.
- July 22, 2009 Applied for extension on rent and continued interviewing candidates.
- August 1, 2009 Based on all applicants responses decided on the best fit based on values. Secured rent money.

Success: Celebrated a successful journey in finding a roommate. Note: My new roommate has many of my values. She has strengths that compliment mine. I think we will become good friends. August 23, 2009.

This example is a brief outline of the decision-making process. Some challenges will be easy and others will be more complex. The key point of the Action Step process is to match values with the decision-making process. It is important to analyze all areas of the SWOT while making decisions because they can affect the outcome. Acting out of character can be critical to successful decisions. For instance, if the person looking for the roommate stated clearly that they value kindness and honesty and they don't seek those characteristics in a roommate, then the efforts to find a good fit will be thwarted. Understanding where you stand on a particular challenge will help you to seek the right answer. Look for solutions that build your character and help you to maintain balance and consistency. Journaling action steps will help you in your decision-making process in the future. It is helpful to journal good and bad outcomes so that you can analyze your successes as well as failures.

CONCLUSION—BUILDING A CLASSROOM WITH COURAGE

Everyone desires to understand who they are and where their future will take them. As teachers and leaders it is our responsibility to understand our own values and how they shape us. When we understand our values we begin to see the picture of the direction of our life. Your classroom can be filled with hope and purpose by teaching a solid foundation of value construction. Here are some steps that you can take that will help your students on a life long journey of productive change. Help your students to get a vision of their own lives by offering a road map that will instill direction.

- ✓ **Step 1:** Talk about values to your students. Help them to recognize what they cherish and what they reject. Offer hope by helping them to see the benefit of values to the decision-making process.
- ✓ **Step 2:** Teach your students to set up a Personal Analysis notebook. Show them how to do a simple SWOT and explain that our strengths and opportunities are the tools that we need to help us overcome challenges. After teaching students how to use the SWOT

give them an assignment that will allow them to use their SWOT as a tool to solve the problem presented.

✓ **Step 3:** Get personal. Follow up with students personally and find out what they value. Teach them to cherish the gifts and talents that they've been given. Foster hope by helping them to see that they are unique and have a special purpose.

Offering hope is not a casual process. It is an intentional undertaking that requires attention to the details that make us unique. As a leader, your attention to your own values will affect the lives of your followers. The values that you instill will help students to recognize their own need to tend their particular garden of hope. Use your tools to tend your own life and teach others to use the tools that we offer throughout this book. You have the power of positive change. Use it!

3

Rein in the Rebel

Rekindling Hope

Kind words can be short and easy to speak, but their echoes are truly endless.
~Mother Teresa

STRATEGY: IGNITE FORGIVENESS

THE DILEMMA OF THE REBEL

Linda Bates (fictitious name) taught in school for 11 years. She won a number of teaching awards and was admired by a multitude of students and colleagues. She never missed the annual teacher's conference. This year was no exception. She looked forward to the luncheon group that typically gathered to swap "teacher tales." The stories almost always left her feeling uplifted with a sense of satisfaction that her career was on the right track. It was usually the same clique of teachers that met but this year a new teacher joined them. The conversation started with the predictable funny classroom anecdotes. During a lull in the conversation, Penny the new teacher, raised an issue.

"Since you are all veteran teachers, I have a question. This is my second year of teaching but I find myself getting really burned out on the rebels in the classroom. I have tried all standard methods to get their interest and I'm successful at keeping a modicum of order. But to me, it seems like the rebels are winning. It's getting harder and harder for me to teach the 'hard to teach' students. I feel that I'm losing sight of the reason for which I started teaching. I feel a little angry that I spend so much time trying to reach them that it's taking away my passion." Penny's face was red and she looked at everyone nervously. "Do any of you feel that way?"

Linda patted Penny's arm. "Penny, don't take it so hard. All of us understand what you are going through." The group bobbed their heads in agreement. "I don't let the trouble-makers get to me. I decided a long time ago that I can't save the world, so I concentrate my best efforts on the students who have real potential."

"I agree," Jack added. "It's been my experience that most of the rebels come from rough home environments. Some of their parents act the exact same way. My philosophy is to ignore the trouble-makers. Spend your time on the kids that will succeed. You're always going to have the rebels in your classroom, so your best hope is to manage them and don't worry about the ones that you can't reach."

Allison chimed in. "I don't know about that philosophy Jack. I feel that I have a responsibility to reach the rebels."

Linda added, "I think that we all want to help the hard-to-reach students Allison. But I can't waste time on students that are not interested in learning. I like to leave those students to the professionals. I quickly refer my difficult students to special programs and sometimes they can get help there. I think I've been a successful teacher because I spend my time teaching students who really want to learn. You've worked very hard to get where you are. Don't let those types ruin your career. Just like you said, you are already burning out. Don't make it so hard on yourself."

Linda left the luncheon wondering if she had given the right advice. She began to think about some of the students that she shunned over the years. She wondered where they were today and if they ever found happiness and success. She shrugged off the feeling of guilt, rationalizing that if you focus on the rebels, they will just make more trouble.

Teachers have a profound impact on how their students see themselves. As we explored in Chapter 1, the concept of "self" leads one to develop their values. Everyone passes through troubled waters at some point in their life. Students are no different. Many of them come to the classroom with cheery smiles and wearing the latest fashions. But beneath the veneer of confidence lie broken hearts and fearful souls. Take a close look and you'll likely find that contrary to adult belief, your students are anxious about their futures and worried about past failures and successes. They see you, the teacher, and wonder: Who is this person standing in front of me? How will she or he treat me? Will I be able to understand what's being taught? Will I fail or succeed? These are natural questions that the students ask as they enter your classroom. What this says is that the classroom can be an ideal place to offer hope. Pick up the challenge. Let your class know that A.I.D. is on the way! In this case, A.I.D. is a compound response to an expressed need. As a transformational leader what you can offer your students is the power of **A**ffirmation, **I**nformation, and **D**irection.

GIVING A.I.D.

A—Affirmation

Almost every student has a story to tell about a teacher who either impacted their lives positively or sent them on a journey of self-doubt and fear. Teachers have a powerful opportunity to influence and affect their students for good or for ill. Words and deeds really can make or break a student. Encouragement and praise, like condemnation and criticism shape and affect behavior (Covey, 2004: 133). This is especially true of students who are, for one reason or the other, classified as disruptive or rebels. We all know who these students are or at least we convince ourselves that we do.

Affirmation is a positive declaration. Positive declarations need to be authentic. They do not include false declarations that sound good but are not true. Providing effective feedback can be a powerful tool if it is framed correctly. Feedback answers a simple question. "How am I doing?" Some students expect negative feedback because it is the path that they are used to. They might have been bombarded with self-doubt because of the specific pattern of negative self-talk that has been prevalent because of past failures.

The language of negative self-talk is the opposite of affirmation. It is everywhere. If you refer back to your SWOT you will see that some of the negative self-talk exists in you. As you prepared your section on WEAKNESSES, did you find yourself delving into a darker side of your character? The dark side often comes from the inability to see the strengths that counter balance the flaws that often others have convinced us that we have.

After beginning your SWOT analysis, you are in a better position to offer A.I.D. to others. Your SWOT has shown that your strengths have linkages. In the analysis of your SWOT you no doubt discovered that you have positive attributes that will truly give authentic affirmation to your circumstances. Authentic affirmation results from analyzing your circumstances and recognizing that you have specific tools that you can apply that will help you to find positive and harmonious outcomes.

To offer affirmation is more than a complement or subtly acknowledging another person's existence. Teaching with the tool of affirmation is the most effective way to help others to evaluate and give long-lasting feedback that is generated by the self rather than others. Affirmation can serve as a tool when you show students how to effectively evaluate their own particular strengths. As you teach them to evaluate their strengths in your classroom you will endeavor to uncover the specific strengths of the rebels. Doing a specific SWOT in your classroom will help them to become creative in problem solving issues and assignments. The SWOT is particularly helpful in identifying teams and teaching effective team behavior.

As you discover strengths in your students, you will have a clear grasp on an effective way to affirm them and to add to their successes in your class. By teaching people to simply evaluate their own SWOT they will find answers that are specific to their needs. While everyone is uniquely made up of unique sets of circumstances in their lives, the best person to find true affirmation is the self. Self-affirmation consists of understanding your strengths and neutralizing your weaknesses through resources and opportunities that present themselves.

When people constantly seek affirmation from others it becomes a crutch. The person who does not have the tools of self-affirmation will seek guidance continually or they will continually rebel. Their view of self becomes distorted by the people that they talk to. This can be a self-destructive force that many have a hard time recognizing. It can be carried on throughout life. Often, it is not recognized for what it is. Building a foundation by showing followers how to work their own self-evaluation is the most exciting affirmation tool because it allows them to search their own values and their own character structure to discover strengths that will help them overcome any areas of self-doubt.

Consider Kim, a 17 year old. Kim has a wonderful family who surrounded her with every advantage a teenager could want. Kim's grandmother doted on her from the time she was a baby. Whatever Kim desired her grandmother provided. Her grandmother's motive was to give Kim everything that she lived without as a child. If Kim had a problem her grandmother attempted to fix it by offering advice, money or things to make her feel better. Kim ran to her grandmother for everything.

In her grandmother's eyes Kim was a delight. She bragged about Kim at all of her social events. If Kim made a mistake her grandmother was there to fix it. One time when Kim was learning to drive she hit another car. She ran to her grandmother for advice. "We don't need to tell your father," the grandmother said. "I'll tell him I was driving and you won't get in trouble. If you tell him that you did it, your father will punish you. There is no sense in that. It was an accident."

As you can imagine Kim was a spoiled girl. Her grandmother thought that her attention would encourage and affirm Kim, and she would turn out strong and wise. Nothing could have been further from the truth. Because she always had a crutch, as Kim relied on her grandmother for everything.

As Kim moved through her school career she didn't have many friends. As she got older, she became withdrawn and took little interest in anything. She didn't show respect for her teachers because her grandmother eschewed any correction that she received over the years. Kim had become an emotional cripple and inwardly she rebelled against anyone who stood in her way. Kim didn't have a clue who she was or what her real strengths were because she lived her life by seeking approval from another person. She saw herself through the eyes of her grandmother and was confused by her lack of self-knowledge.

If you had Kim in your class you could be a true leader to her by helping her to discover her hidden strengths. As you seek ways to make her successful in her own right, you would help to transform her to the person she was created to be. You could help her unlock the long-lasting tool of self-affirmation. You might ask, how?

The first step of affirmation is the SWOT tool. It not only helps a person discover their strengths, it also helps them to uncover their fears, doubts, and insecurities. Uncovering personal character qualities would give Kim the opportunity to analyze her own needs. Show her how to accept challenges using her inner strengths and opportunities through the step-by-step action plan offered in Chapter 1. Affirming another individual is offering hope of managing their own lives successfully. Kim can learn to be her own self-coach and rely less on others to solve her life challenges.

I—Information

While we may commonly define the rebel as the one who interrupts the smooth flow of the classroom, the larger question is how many other potential rebels are out there? We might do well to consider that the rebel may actually be anyone. Even the most quiet and demure people may be cowering under the strain of a rebellious heart, one filled with self-doubt. This is where you have the capacity to set the rebel free by igniting a spirit of forgiveness. We will explore the deeper side of rebellion and how forgiveness plays an integral factor in changing the tide of pain that rebellion causes.

Let's consider how a person might become a rebel. Rebellion comes from self- doubt. It is a form of protection that anyone can develop to say, "Leave me alone, I'm not like you." We all have a form of rebellion when we sense that we are not like others. If we see that we are in circumstances that challenge our thinking we will set up a protective outer covering to hide our hurt, pain, or fear. This protection is natural. When it becomes destructive is that point when we harm ourselves through rebellion. We may also intentionally or unintentionally harm others. We've all experienced the effects of another person's rebellion and we may be a victim of our own rebellion. So how can you deliver hope to yourself or others when you recognize rebellion? The answer is simple—ignite forgiveness.

The best way to ignite forgiveness is to have accurate information. What is the root of rebellion? Rebellion comes from the act of holding onto or carrying around a feeling of resentment and grievance. Resentment can come in many forms. It can come from simply thinking that another person is more attractive or more entertaining. It can come from a wrong that another person did to you that is hard to forgive and release.

The moment we take an offense and hold it tightly, it changes form. The act of wrapping our brain around resentment allows it to be packed tighter against other similar resentments. Soon, it takes on a form of its own. It is like a snowball. Consider the snowflake effect.

The Snowflake Effect

Did you ever watch snow come down? A snowflake is beautiful and actually consists of water vapor. By itself a snowflake is barely noticeable. When many snowflakes accumulate, they glom together and become heavier. If you gather a lot of snow in your hands and pack it tightly, the snow will condense and the water molecules will join to form hard ice. The ice becomes so dense that the vaporous snowflake changes form. The simple snowflake becomes harder, colder and more difficult to penetrate. The more the snowflakes glom on to this mass, the larger it gets. If there is a deliberate act of packing the snowflakes together to make a snowball there is no limit to the size that it can become. The larger the snowball the more formidable it is. The snowball can actually be destructive if it comes in contact with a mass that is less dense than itself. If the ice is melted, it can again return to a vaporous state. It will never be a snowflake again because the crystals have been broken. Its original structure has been altered. There is a wonderful thing about the melted snowball. Even though it will never again be exactly like its original form, it takes on a different form. When it is melted into water it can have many life-giving opportunities.

Do you understand the metaphor, "resentments attract other resentments and pack together forming a hard core of pain and justification?" The more dense the pain the more destructive it can become. Forgiveness is a way to melt the pain. The information that you can offer yourself and others will break the density of painful living. Here is some information that can help you understand the inner workings of the forgiveness process.

To move forward you will need a few simple tools. It will be up to you if you want to change your thinking. For some the act of change will be difficult. For others, the act of changing your thought pattern will be as simple as holding the snowball up to the warmth of the light and letting it melt. The point is this—before you can help others to transform, you must transform yourself. Your ability to teach and lead require you to master your own resentments. When others see that you are free from pain, they will listen to you. Everyone, to some degree, is carrying resentment about offenses. Why not take the step to free yourself today? Don't just take the steps to change for yourself. Take them so that you can free others.

Challenge Your Thinking

Before we get started you should realize that the initial few exercises are private. They are your private thoughts and your private struggle. Drawing others in on your private struggle will not help you to conquer the problem. In fact it may even hinder your progress because no one else will view the situation exactly like you do. Keep our example of Kim in your mind. Running to another person to solve your problems will not make you strong. Using the tools that you are given will help you to build your own strong foundation.

This exercise may take time depending on the amount of pain you carry. Recognize your painful thoughts for what they are so that you are able to conquer your resentments effectively. They will free you from some of the weaknesses you identified in your SWOT.

Exercise 1—Letting Go

Find a place where you can be completely alone. You should have a quiet space in which you can think and meditate. Number the left-hand-side of a notebook page. Think about the circumstances that bother you. These may be things that bother you from time to time, or take up most of your day. Use one word that describes the offense that causes you to carry resentment and anger. Here are some examples of how your page should be set up:

- Harmful gossip: Heard that untruths were being spread about my relationship with James.
- Friend betrayal: Susan told others about my break-up with James.
- Turned down for promotion: Passed over for the third time.

Write down as many of the offenses that come to mind. Notice that many of these hurts resulted in other related resentments. Also write down what about these offenses still make you angry.

After you have worked on your list, imagine that these painful situations are like the snowflakes. You are free to let each of these melt away right now. There are several things that you can do to release them.

- You can pray and ask for help to let them go.
- You can write them down on little pieces of paper and bury them. Tell yourself that they are no longer a part of your life.
- You can write them out on separate pieces of paper and carefully burn them. Again, telling yourself that they are no longer a part of your life.

Every time the painful thoughts of resentment come up in your mind, remember that you have taken the time to let them go. They no longer have room in your mind. They are no longer going to control your thinking patterns.

The physical act of processing your thoughts will help you to gain control. As you begin to feel the resentment again, remember that you have given yourself permission to walk free. Some of you may say, "But you don't know what this person did to me." You are right. That is why this is a private matter. What these people or thoughts of resentment did in the past they are still doing if you are still thinking about them. It will only end when you bring it to a close.

If you are in a circumstance that a person is holding you captive with abusive actions, you need to seek help to get physically away from the situation before you can begin to heal. The purpose of this exercise is to help you heal from the past.

You have probably heard the saying, "the past is the past." This is true. The present is not the past unless you drag it with you. The world was designed so that each new day is a new beginning. Use this information to ignite forgiveness. Literally, you can ignite your forgiveness by setting the offense out of your life. We certainly wouldn't want to dredge up a person that was dead. We certainly don't want the dead things in our life to walk around with us. Dragging old circumstances is like dragging around the dead. Let them go.

Exercise 2—Living Free

This exercise will also require you to find a place to be alone to meditate. You will use another sheet of paper and set up the left side with numbers. Make a list of things that you would like to do with your life as a person free of the pain of the past. If you find yourself reverting back to old resentful thoughts, go back to Exercise 1. You may need to repeat Exercise 1 many times before you can move on to Exercise 2. As you begin to write down the things that you would like to do with your life, notice how many times painful thoughts will come to mind. If you think of something that you would like to do and the voice of doubt is stopping you from reaching your goal, then these voices are old resentments which must be released.

After you've written a list of your greatest desires for your future, analyze them. In one column put all the things that you can begin to enjoy within the next six months. In another column make a list of things that you can begin to enjoy in a year. In another list, place all of the things that you might enjoy in the next five years. This is the beginning of your goals. Free from the pain of the past—you are free to give your future a delighted, happy, and healthy beginning. You no longer harbor the thoughts that kept you from achieving your goals. You have taken the root of bitterness and yanked it out of the garden of your life.

Exercise 3—Staying Free

The physical act of Exercise 1 and Exercise 2 is important and **very** private. If you draw others in on your process, you may find that they will cripple you from making progress. The key to staying free is to conquer resentment as it crops up. Every day someone commits an offense that could cause resentment. If your receptors are very fine-tuned, you may find that there are dozens of things every day that offend or hurt you deeply. Like the snowball, if you catch the flake early and melt it, it won't get packed hard in your mind. Write the offense down and tell yourself that you will let it go. In the beginning, you may have to do this a lot to conquer your feelings. After some time, you will be able to let offenses roll off of you easily. Your days will be free to concentrate on the goals that you continually set with the free space in your mind.

Exercise 4—Are You the Bully?

Sometimes in your meditation you may think of pain that you have caused. When your mind is free of the thoughts that plague you about what others have done, you may remember what you have done to cause others to hold resentment. This is hard to face, but if you are to be resentment-free and living freely, you must face the seeds of hurt that you've planted. If the circumstance that you caused makes you feel a bit like laughing or it causes you joy then you have become like the hard packed snowball. You are the ice that can cause the pain to someone. This is a root that will also hurt you because it is unrecognized evil. This type of bullying causes others to resent you. It will keep you from realizing your goals because you will find that others will not cooperate with you. The other way that you look at the pain you've caused may make you feel shame and guilt. This also will keep you from moving into a healthy state of mind. Either way, there is a solution to freedom.

- Pray and ask for forgiveness.
- Look at the names and circumstances on the list. Do you still have contact with these people? There are two things that you can do. You may write a little note acknowledging the situation and admit your mistake. The second thing that you can do is to approach the person and acknowledge your mistake personally. Note that you do not have to elaborate or justify your actions. Acknowledge that you were wrong and that you are sorry. Your freedom does not need a forgiving response from them. If you think that you will hurt them with your presence, opt to write the note. Either way you will feel that you have set yourself free from hurting others purposefully. It will help you conquer this type of behavior in future.
- If you are unable to contact the people on your list, make a list of things that you will not do in the future to hurt others. Every time you find yourself doing something on your "will not do" list, recognize it and correct it by saying that you are sorry.

The reason that these exercises work is that they help you to have more freedom than you ever had before. Sometimes it is hard to face the things that cause you pain. If you can face them you will look back with relief and look forward with hope.

As a transformational leader you can help others achieve this freedom by counseling them to:

- let go of resentment;
- forgive people who have caused pain and fear;
- conquer resentment as it starts; and
- free yourself of causing pain to others.

D—Direction

What you have accomplished is a valuable lesson in gaining a sound mind. Leaders need to be free of the constant fear of self-doubt, self-deprecation, and fear. You were created with the ability to make a positive impact on this world. The mere fact that you are reading this book demonstrates your desire to build your own values and help others to build theirs.

Providing direction is helping you and others get on a productive course of change. Goal-setting is the answer to understanding direction. People often rebel from their circumstances because they feel a lack of control. Setting goals for individuals and rewarding progress on the goals is a life-giving force that promotes psychological hardiness. People feel well when they know their life is making progress. Think about the goals that you've set in your life. Imagine the way you feel when you've accomplished a goal that had value to you. Everyone needs direction. Goals are like a roadmap that helps you see the destination. Setting goals that are realistic and time-bound will help you and others to find a course of action (Nelson and Campbell, 2003: 190). In your SWOT notebook set up three pages. Label them:

- Short-term Goals
- One-year Goals
- Five-year Goals

On each page begin to write your goals. An example of a well written goal would look like this:

Short Term Goals
- Write biology assignment by Friday, May 16th.
    - Meet with study team and gather notes by May 8th.
    - Finish gathering library research by May 10th.
    - Make outline by May 11th.
    - Write paper by May 14th.
    - Proof paper and assemble by May 15th.

Goals with detail allow you to take a step-by-step approach in completing the action needed for success. Ambiguous goals are rarely achieved. By placing specific dates for each area of completion you can check your progress and rearrange your schedule to meet the need.

By specifying what you will need to complete the goal, you are allowing yourself reasons to celebrate your successes along the way. Celebrating is an important part of meeting goals because it allows you to mark your success. Keep a log of your goals so that you can improve your motivational skills. When you feel you are procrastinating, review what helped you move forward in the past. Meeting goals is another way to mark an entry in your SWOT under the strength column. You can help others as a transformational leader by:

- showing a follower how to write meaningful goals;
- celebrate with them as they meet their goals. Take an interest in their progress; and
- give support by showing them that their roadmap has value and that they are meeting something far greater than the goal. They are building character and values that are long-lasting and meaningful.

A.I.D. REALIZED

A transformational leader is one who can help others achieve their greatest potential. The ability to help others comes from healthy self-knowledge. If you are a leader who wants to make a difference in the lives of others, you need to be able to communicate clearly. Your clarity will come as you realize your own potential to improve and grow. To recap, here are the few easy steps to offer A.I.D. to others.

1. Affirmation: Help others to see their own strengths through self-evaluation. Teach them to recognize and apply their own worth.
2. Information: Give others the tools to ignite forgiveness. Help them to know that they do not have to be bound by resentment and fear.
3. Direction: Give others direction by teaching them how to make a roadmap of goals. Show them the value of celebrating successes.

You can also help your followers by teaching this formula:

$$\mathbf{F} \text{ (igniting forgiveness)} = \mathbf{A} + \mathbf{I} + \mathbf{D} = \mathbf{H} \text{ (hope)}.$$

What is the personal sacrifice for inculcating forgiveness? It is the act of giving up the hurt and resentment one feels toward others for wrongs committed. It is an act of showing value in others and allowing them the freedom to explore the process of healing. As you exercise your value system, you can demonstrate to your followers that your value system allows you to recognize the good qualities in others. We all have good and bad qualities. Some are able to overcome their supposed bad qualities through the power of forgiveness. Forgiveness means that we are free to start over. Imagine the joy that your students can find in being able to make a new start. What is true for the adult is also true for the student. Forgiveness is liberating.

ONE STEP AT A TIME

In 1992, Kara began teaching at an inner city school in Pittsburgh, Pennsylvania, USA. She left her school late after she volunteered for a tutoring session with some failing students. On her way back to the car Kara was attacked. She couldn't see the face of the person attacking because he was wearing a ski mask that covered his entire face. But Kara saw his eyes.

Kara's attacker was angry and shouted words of racial hate. She fought back vigorously trying her hardest to pull the mask off of her attacker. She was unsuccessful. She was stabbed three times in her left arm and the attacker tried to cut her throat. As Kara began to fall her attacker leaned over her face. She got a clear look at the expression in his eyes. The attack was interrupted when a bus with basketball players pulled into the parking lot. The attacker fled and was not found.

Later, in the hospital, the police questioned Kara. A forensic artist worked with her to reproduce a likeness of her attacker's eyes and other characteristics from his body type. She was questioned about students that may have held resentment against her for one reason or another. That evening, Kara remembered a student who was a rebel in one of her classes. He was always disruptive and resented correction. She remembered a warning that he gave, "If you give me a bad grade, I'll make you regret it." Kara remembered his eyes. They were the eyes of her attacker.

She thought about the young man all night and wondered how she had failed him in the classroom. She knew that he was a rebel and she resented his behavior of disrupting her teaching every day. She recalled the poor marks that she gave him without reaching out to him with help. But there was something more that she remembered that caused her the most pain. Kara remembered the student's comments on one of his tests. It read, "I'm failing this stupid class because nobody cares!"

The hard facts were there. Kara really hadn't cared about her student. She knew from the first day of class that he carried a chip on his shoulder. She chose to ignore it. Her strategy was to ignore bad behavior and hope for the best with the students who were learning. In the midst of Kara's physical pain she recognized her own failure to reach out to a human being who was hurting.

It wasn't because Kara didn't care about her students. She really did. What she didn't know how to do was to reach out to all of her students in a way that was meaningful to them. She thought of it as a problem that would go away. Now she realized that her problem was much deeper.

The next day Kara identified her attacker and the student was arrested. He pled guilty and was put in jail. Kara saw this as an opportunity to right a number of wrongs. Her first step was to realize that she had a weakness as a teacher. She failed to care for students that she was uncomfortable with. She knew that her actions didn't line up with her values. Here, she saw an opportunity.

Kara met with her attorney. "I have a plan to help this boy," she explained. "I would like to offer my services to the court to tutor him and others in prison."

The attorney had his doubts but Kara persisted. The court met with the boy's attorney and made the offer. The first meeting was awkward. Kara began to tell her story slowly to the boy. Her eyes welled with tears as she faced her attacker again.

"I'm sorry for the pain that I helped cause in your life. I know that as a teacher I should have been more concerned with your needs as a student."

The boy looked at her with astonishment. "Why are you apologizing to me?", he asked. His voice was shaking.

"I'm apologizing for my part in your pain," Kara said simply.

"What do you want from me?" the boy asked. "Am I supposed to apologize to you? Don't you think I'm taking my punishment?"

Kara smiled. "I am not asking for an apology. I'm offering to tutor you while you're in prison so that when you come out you will be on track with your education. I'm offering you an opportunity to be released from your pain."

The boy couldn't believe what he was hearing. "I have to think about it," he said sheepishly. "Will you come back next week and we can talk about it?"

That week Kara also did some soul searching. She wrote down some of the values that she held as a leader. She recognized that she let the pressures of her job and fears overtake her greatest desires. She wrote this statement:

I will recognize that all of my students have worth. I believe in the value of forgiveness.

(July, 1992)

This wasn't an easy statement for Kara to write. She bore the scars of her attack both mentally and physically. But she knew that her life could not move forward if she couldn't come to terms with her own resentment, pride, fears, and anger. She purposed in her heart to change.

The next week Kara returned to the prison. The boy was anxious to see her. He grinned as she approached with guards at both of their sides.

"I'm going to take you up on your offer," he said. "I've given it a lot of thought and if you can ask me to forgive you, I certainly need to ask for your forgiveness."

Kara tutored the boy successfully for one year. There was a great change that came over both of them in the process. For Kara, the act of forgiveness took on special meaning as she took the first step to right a wrong that had been committed toward her. It wasn't her responsibility to do so but her values called her to take a step out of her comfort zone. She allowed her life to be interrupted by an opportunity that would have lasting results.

For the boy, the act of forgiveness took on great meaning. Instead of returning from prison with a life filled with hate and resentment; he emerged whole. He had a hard time embracing the fact that he had been forgiven because it was not a value that he was familiar with. As a result of Kara's patient kindness, his life was changed forever.

DEFINING AND MEASURING SUCCESS

Reining in the rebel isn't a short journey. It's a process that may not come as easily as in our example. It takes time. Many people find it hard to accept that they have been forgiven and experience setbacks of self-doubt and self-deprecation. This is natural. The "rebel" label is hard to lift. Change can be a painfully slow process which is why transformational teachers must commit to a winning strategy, believing that change will come. Pointing the student toward a desired and hopeful future communicates the teacher's belief that the anticipated change tomorrow is worth every ounce of effort today.

We've all heard stories about teachers who held true to their commitments, never gave up on their students, and many years later heard from students who had made a success of their lives. The students often recall the teacher's belief in them which they say stayed with them long after they left the classroom. If you're looking for a potent measure of transformational teaching, this is it. Success isn't as elusive as you first thought. Here are two clear ways to define it. First, as you demonstrate that you have the ability to forgive, you will notice that you are released from your own resentment and bitterness. As you let go of the rope of anger you can recognize that your values are in action. Action values have purpose. They move you to a place of change in your own heart. They allow you to see the best in others and seek the highest good in others.

The second way to define success is to see it in others. Recognize little wins as significant. Little wins lead to bigger wins. Remember the football game? The big prize does not come until the Super Bowl. Each win pushes the team toward the greater prize. It takes a team to win. No one player does it all on their own. As you help your student to recognize little wins they will become more confident in their ability to get to the Super Bowl of their life. Goal-setting is a tool that helps students recognize that little wins are opportunities to build their own value system (Covey, 2004: 194). These are teachable moments that cement solid values in their lives. The dual benefit is that in these same moments your own values are reinforced and hope is given a general boost.

CONCLUSION—BUILDING A CLASSROOM WITH HOPE

The following tools help ignite forgiveness. These steps of change take on new meaning for your own value statement and give you the personal freedom to mine for action values that communicate hope.

- ✓ **Step 1:** Recognize that we are all created to be different from one another.
- ✓ **Step 2:** In your personal SWOT book write out the opportunities that you recognize as demonstrating the strategy of forgiveness.

✓ **Step 3:** In your Strength Section, list events in your life that you experienced forgiveness.

✓ **Step 4:** In your Threat Section, list what might happen if you don't offer forgiveness. Be specific. Recognize that you have the power to hold yourself accountable for your own actions.

✓ **Step 5:** In your Weaknesses Section, list areas that define vulnerability.

Analyze you entries. You may notice that your values are opportunities to be creative. Watch and wait for timely affirmative action. Ask yourself, "What information do I have that will help my student to overcome weakness in their lives? What can I offer them to give them new direction?" Igniting forgiveness is an ongoing strategy. It becomes the hope that allows the transformational teacher to recognize and redirect the act and spirit of defiance in others as well as in self.

4

Truth or Consequences

We know truth, not only by reason, but also by the heart.

~Blaise Pascal

STRATEGY: LAUNCH THE 3 R'S—RELIABILITY, RESPECT, AND REPUTATION

MORAL FORTITUDE

Morality is deeply personal. It is so personal that how one thinks and conducts themselves will affect the outcomes of most situations. Not only do personal morals affect an individual's circumstances, they also affect others. Morals have long reaching effects that can change the course of history.

What is a moral? The word moral comes from the Latin word *moralis* which means manner, character or proper behavior. The concept of morality can easily be argued and has been for centuries across all cultures. So to devise a list of what is proper behavior would be somewhat ludicrous considering that what is proper in one culture may be entirely improper in another. However, the concept of individual moral fortitude can be easily understood throughout the world. All people know that character drives society. We cannot live in the world without the semblance of order. Order boils down to how our actions affect others. How we govern our personal behavior paints a picture about who we are deeply and our intentions. Each person chooses a set of values that determine right or wrong based on their religion, society, family and friends (Kouzes and Posner, 2002: 54–56).

Before we continue in the discussion of how your morals affect others we would like you to answer a few questions. Answer the questions honestly.

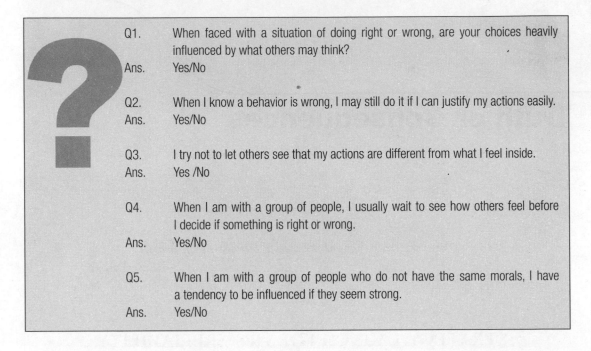

Q1.	When faced with a situation of doing right or wrong, are your choices heavily influenced by what others may think?	
Ans.	Yes/No	
Q2.	When I know a behavior is wrong, I may still do it if I can justify my actions easily.	
Ans.	Yes/No	
Q3.	I try not to let others see that my actions are different from what I feel inside.	
Ans.	Yes /No	
Q4.	When I am with a group of people, I usually wait to see how others feel before I decide if something is right or wrong.	
Ans.	Yes/No	
Q5.	When I am with a group of people who do not have the same morals, I have a tendency to be influenced if they seem strong.	
Ans.	Yes/No	

How did you answer? If you answered "no" to most of these questions you probably do have strong moral fortitude. Strong moral fortitude comes from a pre-determined sense of right and wrong and a willingness to stand firm on your convictions. Standing firm on your convictions is vital in leadership. As you stand firm you build character. If you want to garner the trust of your followers you will have to have a belief system that carries you through times of adversity. Your convictions should not easily be swayed even in the face of peer pressure. Most importantly your sense of what is good and right should carry you through all of your decision-making processes.

WHO CARES?

Jack taught for fifteen years in a private school. He loved the school because they had a high moral code for the teachers as well as the students. When hired, each teacher had to sign a strict code of ethics statement. The statement included a section for grading. A grading rubric was issued to every teacher to ensure fairness. Each year the faculty reviewed the code and everyone signed it as they renewed their teaching contract.

Gar, a student in Jack's Calculus class, struggled the entire year with his grades. Jack even arranged for a private tutor to help Gar succeed but he was not able to complete the work to the school's standards. Gar was a star athlete and was considered by scouts to be a potential for scholarship to a well known university. It was a feather in the private school's cap to have such a renowned player who was making weekly headlines in the newspapers.

One afternoon the headmaster cornered Jack in the hallway. "I'd like to see you in my office later today to discuss Gar's mid-term grades. Please bring your grade book to the meeting and any documentation that you have on his scores." Jack agreed and gathered all of the required documents.

When he arrived in the headmaster's office he was surprised to see several other teachers present. "We have a problem," Mr Otis, the headmaster, said to the teachers. "As you know our funding relies on our schools performance. Each of you as teachers are required to help all of the students succeed. This school has benefited from the athletic ability of Gar Parson. He has raised the awareness of the public and for the first time in our twenty year history, our school is being noticed by very influential people. In fact, because of Gar's popularity, his grandfather has offered to build the library that we so desperately need. All of the student's are going to benefit."

All three teachers in the room nodded and smiled at one another. All felt proud that the school was making the progress that they all worked so hard to achieve. Jim Rollins, the head coach spoke. "Gar isn't the only athlete that has been noticed by the scouts. We have the possibility of three or even four of our guys in the news for scholarships."

"That's great news Rollins." Mr Otis said. "Good job!" Rollins smiled and walked toward the back of the room.

"I guess the three of you are wondering why I've called this meeting." Everyone including Jim nodded. "Well there is a fly in the ointment. It seems that Gar as well as the other athletes are failing in your classes. I've asked you all to bring your records. Look them over. I'm sure there is some mistake in your grading."

Jim was the first to speak. "Mr Otis, I've personally worked with Gar to help him and he has a tutor for Calculus. I'm afraid that he doesn't have the aptitude."

Mr Otis spoke again. "You know what it means to have this library for our school and the notoriety that will come from the selection of these young men will have a profound effect on our budget for years to come. I guess what I'm saying is that I want these boys to succeed. Look at your grading and see what you can do. I'll check back with each of you in a few weeks. By the way," he added, "two of you have been nominated to be teacher of the year. I can't say at this point which two but it will go a long way toward your tenure at this school. You're all doing a fine job. Let's make sure these boys get the grades they deserve and we get the funding we need."

Jim knew exactly what Mr Otis was suggesting. He was suggesting that the grades should be altered to show that the students were passing. Jim was disappointed and hurt that Mr Otis would compromise the standards of the school for monetary gain. Later that day Jim cornered another teacher who had been in the meeting. "Alice, what do you think about Mr Otis' suggestion?" He asked, hoping that he would find an ally.

"I've given it a lot of thought." Alice said sheepishly. "Otis is the boss. If that's what it takes to keep our school going, I'm not going to be the one to get in the way. I'm doing what I've been told. Besides, who can it hurt? These guys have a great opportunity ahead of them.

A few bad grades shouldn't hold them back. I want them to succeed. Besides, this is good for all of us. No one is the loser here. Just do what you are told Jim and help this school move forward."

Let's stop this story a moment and take a look at Jim's dilemma. Our individual uniqueness causes us to decide what we will allow in our lives that affects our behavior. How we conform to the standards set before us determines how others view us. This is a loaded statement because we may conform to standards that allow us to be accepted by those around us and yet those around us may be morally bankrupt in terms of society as a whole. So morals, as stated earlier, are deeply personal and should be carefully considered in determining our values.

Jim's dilemma, like many others, is something that we could face. We can either choose to do what we know is right or we can compromise and believe we are doing what others think is right even when it is clearly the wrong choice. Have you ever been faced with a decision like this? Right now, imagine you are Jim. You know that you signed a code of ethics which clearly states the standard of the school. You also know that many students will benefit in multiple ways if you cooperate with the headmaster's suggestion to help students by falsely reporting grades that they didn't earn. You have other teachers (your peers) who are pressuring you to go along with the group's decision to look out for the good of many. However, on the other hand you wonder if the good of many is really good because the gain is received from deceit. What will you choose to do?

There is something even deeper to consider. The headmaster is the leader. He has been charged with upholding the moral stance of the school. The consequences of leadership in

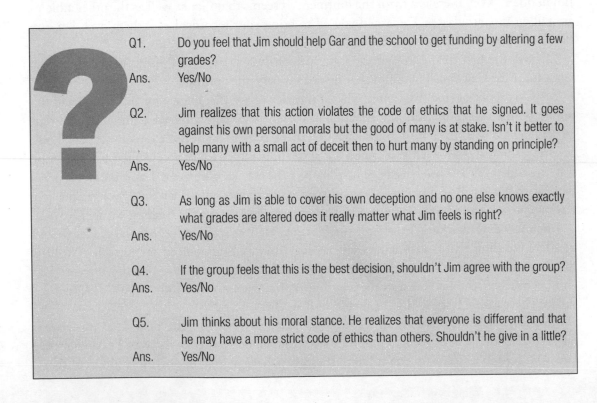

Q1. Do you feel that Jim should help Gar and the school to get funding by altering a few grades?
Ans. Yes/No

Q2. Jim realizes that this action violates the code of ethics that he signed. It goes against his own personal morals but the good of many is at stake. Isn't it better to help many with a small act of deceit then to hurt many by standing on principle?
Ans. Yes/No

Q3. As long as Jim is able to cover his own deception and no one else knows exactly what grades are altered does it really matter what Jim feels is right?
Ans. Yes/No

Q4. If the group feels that this is the best decision, shouldn't Jim agree with the group?
Ans. Yes/No

Q5. Jim thinks about his moral stance. He realizes that everyone is different and that he may have a more strict code of ethics than others. Shouldn't he give in a little?
Ans. Yes/No

this situation are profound. As in all leadership, the moral decisions of the leader affect many. Ethical dilemmas are difficult because the people involved have difficulty making decisions based on their own moral standards (Johnson, 2001). Answer the following questions. They will help you to determine your own values. Immerse yourself in the story and imagine how you would answer in this situation.

How closely are your answers tied in with the questions that you answered previously? Each of the questions are in alignment with the previous questions. Did you alter your answers based on the case and your feelings?

TRUTH

What is truth? Philosophers and scholars have long debated whether truth is subjective, relative, objective or absolute. An easy answer in this case is to believe that truth is subjective. Moral fortitude is to be able to stand on moral ground in the face of difficulties. Why is this important as a leader? Why is truth a factor?

Truth plays a vital role in leadership (Covey, 2004: 35). Followers expect leaders to tell the truth. They expect that leaders will uphold the truth so that they personally can follow safely. If your leader is obviously not truthful then you will have difficulty trusting their actions and reactions to situations. Imagine a leader who continually covers up truth in an effort to find the good for many. Where is the bottom line? Who decides what is good and what is harmful. This notion raises a lot of questions. As in our case above, the leader, Mr Otis, has been given the job of upholding truth for the school. He, as the gatekeeper, holds the responsibility of seeing that the school is safe from financial disaster, ethical bankruptcy and harm from social predators. The essence of his leadership is to ensure that the right decisions are made according the code of honor that stakeholders have entrusted to him. Mr Otis is like many other leaders who are charged with the same tasks. They have tough decisions to make daily about the obvious and not so obvious moral decisions.

The decisions that Mr Otis faced and asked his followers to face comes from a lack of truth. He did not take the time to understand his own value system. To Mr Otis values and truth are relative. That is, he will pick the road that seems will give the most people an opportunity. What Mr Otis failed to see is that his lack of truth will cause greater harm to more people then will be benefited.

Let's break down the harm that Mr Otis has inflicted on his school and the damage that his leadership may cause.

- The code of ethics: The code of ethics is a predetermined document that binds everyone who signs it that they will uphold the truth. It is not arbitrary. It spells out that a distinct set of rules govern that will ensure that all are treated fairly (Maxwell, 2003). By asking the teachers to compromise for the good of many, Mr Otis violated the code that he was entrusted to uphold. His leadership is affected because the people that signed the code know that is meaningless. Mr Otis cannot be trusted to make sound decisions for the school.

- Decision-making: As a key decision maker, Mr Otis demonstrated that he lacks credibility. He lost his voice in clarifying future values because he is not morally competent. His decisions will be questioned because he failed to be in alignment with his commitment to sound leadership.
- Win/lose: Mr Otis felt that he was seeking a win-win situation by altering a few grades. He actually created a losing situation for all involved. By choosing deceit he will not be able to create a spirit of community. He has divided his community and put them in danger so that no one is truthfully accountable for the well-being of all of the students.
- Commitment: As a leader it is important to have a sound commitment from followers who support the governing practices of the organization. Followers who see leaders sabotage the organization's government will abandon their commitment to the organization and to the leader. Mr Otis did great long term harm to the school by demonstrating that he cared more for money then he did for the well-being if individuals. He placed is followers at risk by asking them to sacrifice their dignity and honor as fair leaders of students.
- Vision: Mr Otis painted a clear vision of the future to his followers. What his followers saw was a vision of dishonesty, compromise, incompetence and risk. Instead of creating a safe environment for followers, Mr Otis demonstrated that the future was bleak. In a single stroke of poor judgment and lack of firm values, the school moved potentially to a future of strife.

The truth is hard to uphold at times. Truth can seem relative but a leader that defines their values ahead of time will have the tools to chose the path of moral fortitude. A truthful leader with sound values will lead people in a direction that engenders confidence. Followers will not have confidence in a deceitful leader. Leaders who have proven skills in choosing the high ground, even though the path may not lead to an immediate reward, will gain the respect of their followers (Caroselli, 2000: 51).

THE 3 R'S—RELIABILITY, RESPECT, AND REPUTATION

This next exercise will help you to analyze another portion of your SWOT (strengths, weaknesses, opportunity and threats). We are going to explore how the 3 R's can help you to be a strong transformational leader.

In your SWOT notebook start three pages. Label the first page RELIABILITY. Label the second page RESPECT and the third page REPUTATION.

On the first page labeled RELIABILITY, make a column on the left side and label it: How I Rely on Others. On the right hand side make a column and label it: How I am Reliable.

On the second page labeled RESPECT make a column on the left-hand-side and label it: Respect for Myself. On the right side make a column and label it Respect for Others.

On the third page labeled REPUTATION make a column on the left-hand-side and label it: My Positive Reputation. On the right side make a column and label it My Challenged Reputation.

Now that you've set up your notebook we will examine your ability to be reliable. Reliability is the degree that you can be depend upon. If you consider our previous case you can probably point out flaws in Mr Otis' reliability. He may at one point been a reliable leader but as soon as he suggested that followers act dishonestly, he compromised his dependability.

Dependability is a key motivator for followers. People want to know that their leaders have the competence to make decisions and to follow through with confidence. Have you ever considered how you rely on your leaders to make decisions that will offer safety and ensure a future of hope?

When people feel that a leader is reliable they automatically have hope. What are they hoping for? They have hope that the leader will understand change and that through change they will have a sense of stability. The stability that a leader offers is twofold. First followers look for consistency. Consistency requires emotional intelligence. Communicating a safe environment where standards are clear is the first step in creating balance (Mathis and Jackson, 2006: 60). The second way a leader offers stability is creating a spirit of community. When followers feel that they are a part of a greater vision and the vision includes their skills and talents they feel motivated to contribute. Followers that are relied on are as much a factor in the success of an organization as leaders who demonstrate their dependability. Dependability is a symbiotic state that breeds motivation. It has to be fostered and it has to be recognized.

In your SWOT notebook on the page RELIABILITY consider the people that you rely on for your success. Think about everyone in your life that helps you move forward. In the left hand column under How I Rely on Others make a list of the people that you rely on in your personal and professional life. Across from their name add in one or two words how you rely on them. For example:

Sister Sue: Friend
Boss Bill: Leader-mentor
Husband Dan: Emotional support provider

List everyone in your life that has significance and recognize their contributions to your life balance. Recognizing them will help you to see the importance they play in your ability to be a leader. Identifying their role will also help you in the second part of this study. After you've listed all the people that you can think of and recognize their roles; start the second section on the right hand column labeled: How I am Reliable. In this column, write down all the ways in which you can be depended upon. Across from the list of dependable acts, write the names or places of service that you affect. For example:

Coach: Coach daughter's drama club

Teacher: Teach second grade

Mother: Take care of family

After you've completed your lists recognize your strengths and transfer them to the STRENGTHS section of your SWOT. As you examine your list take note of the areas, of reliability that you know needs, improvement and transfer those needs into your WEAKNESSES or OPPORTUNITY sections of your SWOT.

By analyzing your dependability factor you will see that your leadership is stronger in areas that you may not have considered. Your role as a dependable person is vital in the lives of others. Just as you've been given hope by the people that you can depend on, you are also giving hope to others.

YOUR LANDSCAPE—RELIABILITY

From your point of view how do you fare? Do others see you as reliable? Most people would look at their list and feel very good about their reliability factor. But there is a deeper side of reliability that may challenge your leadership capabilities. After reading the following story, try to pick out how you might react.

Rachel was a new teacher hired at Thompson Elementary School. She was slim, very pretty, single, and full of life. She was the first new teacher the school had in seven years. The school had a reputation of long tenure for their teachers. Rachel was hired to teach the first grade. It was a dream job and she was excited to start the year. She had high hopes for making new friends and beginning a wonderful career.

On the first day the Assistant Principal, Allison showed Rachel around the school. She introduced her to the other teachers who were setting up their classrooms. School would start in a week and there was much to be done. Everyone greeted her as they stopped by each room but Rachel noticed that no one said more than a quick hello.

"I just want to give you a little heads up." The Assistant Principal, Allison said. "People in this school don't like change. They really liked the former first grade teacher but she didn't work out if you know what I mean."

Rachel shook her head. "What do you mean?"

"I mean, she wasn't one of us." Allison said. "Let's just leave it at that. You may find that people won't trust you. You are new so don't let it upset you."

Rachel was disappointed to hear this but thought that the news didn't really apply to her. She knew that she had a good reputation. Whatever the problem, it was not really any of her concern. At least that is what she told herself.

At lunch time the teachers gathered in the teacher's lounge. Rachel joined them. "Your rooms are shaping up nicely," she said. To her dismay no one responded. She waited silently for someone else to talk but for twenty minutes everyone sat silent. Finally she broke the silence. "Is anything wrong?" she asked trying to smile.

"Nothing is wrong," one of the teachers said. They all cleaned their lunches from the table and left the room.

Rachel was disturbed. She wasn't sure how to handle the chilly response from her co-workers. Her decision was to watch and wait. For the entire next week the response was the same. As she tried to reach out to specific teachers she was given quick answers and it was apparent that people tried to avoid her. Near the end of the week she made an appointment with Mr Marken, the principal.

"I wanted to thank you for offering me this job. I'm very excited to teach here and I'm looking forward to this school year. I do have a little bit of a challenge that I would like to address and wonder if you can offer me any advice." Rachel went on to tell about the cold response she was getting from others.

"I wouldn't let it bother you Rachel. Some of these people like to talk. Rumors aren't always true." Mr Marken said, helping Rachel toward the door.
"What rumor?" Rachel asked. "Are there rumors about me?" She said with an alarmed voice. "Have I done something that I'm not aware of?"
"Like I said," Mr Marken continued showing Rachel out of his office. "Don't let it concern you. Do your job."

Rachel left confused and hurt. She could feel the cold response from her co-workers. For months people would only speak to her if she asked a question. Her heart was heavy and her dream job turned sour before it even really began.

Near the end of the first semester Mr Marken called Rachel into his office. "I'm sorry to tell you that we won't be able to renew your contract next year. It isn't working out for you here Rachel. Others don't feel that you are a good fit at our school.
Tears welled in Rachel's eyes. "Do parents think that I'm not a good fit?"
"I've not heard anything from parents except many are concerned that you don't look as happy as a first grade teacher should look."

The end of the year ended just as it had started and on the last day Rachel felt so disappointed that she could hardly breathe. Not one teacher reached out to her and offered her hope. Not one person could give her a reason why she was not accepted. Her heart was broken.

What Rachel did was very exciting. Instead of falling into deep despair she took hold of what she knew to be the truth. Everyone at the school tried to make her feel as if she was the reason for their coldness. She spent time analyzing the situation and wrote the facts on a piece of paper. Rachel listed what she knew and faced her values. One of the things that she valued about herself was her ability to be reliable. In the face of day to day confusion and hurt she remained reliable to the task that she had before her. She taught with her best abilities and continued the course.

Others in this story were reliable as well. They relied on their values. Their values were weak and they could not stand without the aid of other's opinions. As false rumors started, no one took the time to find out the truth. They could be relied on to stand on the side of ignorance.

Rachel never knew the reason for other's behavior. She could only hold on to her own values as she moved on.

This may seem like a harsh story. Even though the names have been changed, it is a true story. This story has an important point. The act of reliability has two sides. You should examine your values and understand what it is that you can be relied on to do. Can others sway you to do wrong? Can you be relied on to stand for what is right even when it is difficult? You will have to choose what your value of reliability means to you as it will certainly spell out the next most important value and that is respect.

YOUR LANDSCAPE—RESPECT

How do you define respect? We have given you two stories where reliability and respect have been challenged. The key factor in understanding reliability, respect, and reputation is that they are not just words. They are action words. Almost every circumstance that you face will require you to act with one or all of these concepts coming into play.

Here are some ideas for you to consider about respect. You may add your own to the list. Respect is:

- Loving yourself
- Caring about others
- Being trustworthy
- Listening
- Honesty
- Truthfulness
- Honor

The fact is that respect comes from a deep-seated value that stands for what is right and believes that it is worth the pain of holding fast to what you believe to be true. This value is one of the greatest values. It is one that is hard to uphold because it causes you to stand up in the face of opposition at times. It can also cause you to be very unpopular with others.

In your SWOT on your RESPECT page make a column and label it: How I respect myself. On the other side of the page make a column and label it: What I respect in others. This page can change your life. It will help you to see the depth of who you are. This will affect your decisions from here on because you will intentionally know how you will act in difficult situations. After you've spent time on this page go back and review the first story and answer these questions. Sometime in the near future you will be faced with a dilemma. After answering these questions and considering your stance of reliability and respect in your SWOT, you will clearly know what to do and how you will garner your own respect. First and foremost, respect yourself.

1. Do I follow a code of ethics?
2. Do I have a clear sense of right and wrong?

3. Will I stand up for what I believe to be truth?
4. Can I rely on myself to do the right thing?

YOUR LANDSCAPE—REPUTATION

Reputation is an outcome of reliability and respect. Think of a great leader in history. What do you remember from what you learned about their reputation? Your reputation is your legacy. Who you are and who you are remembered as will be the result of the moment to moment decisions that you make to take a particular action. Actions add up to reputation.

Others may come and try to tarnish your reputation but in the long run they cannot if you hold on to your values. This is the bottom line why it is vital to know how you will react before a circumstance occurs. Your balance requires you to have a clear understanding of who you are and where you are going.

Transformational leaders are effective when they are consistent with their values. The moment you falter there are people that are ready to discredit you. Even if you didn't do anything to cause a situation, as in the case of Rachel, people will still try to discredit you. This is the fallen nature of human beings. You can't stop this but there is a powerful tool that you can develop to combat negative attacks. That is, be true to yourself.

CHANGING YOUR LANDSCAPE

Suppose that you are Mr Otis, the headmaster in the first story. Just for a moment imagine that you were the one that made the decision to take the low road and ask others to do a less then ethical act. You go home after asking others to cheat and lie and it bothers you. In fact you realize that what you are does not really please you. You try to justify yourself in your own eyes and say that it is for the good of many. But deep inside you've lost respect for yourself. In fact you know that you are not a really ethical person.

Or imagine that you are one of the teachers that listens to gossip and rumors about Rachel. You allow others to dictate your behavior. You feel bad that Rachel is shunned for no truthful reason and you even know that the person spreading the gossip is known to lie. You fear that you will be ostracized from your peers if you don't join the group. It doesn't please you and deep inside you know it is wrong. You justify yourself by saying that everyone can't be wrong. Can you change?

If you are reading this and something is deeply nagging you then it is time to change your course. If you don't change your course you risk your entire life's message. Everyone around you will know the truth and you will leave this world with little satisfaction. There are people waiting on you to be a person of integrity. They are hoping that you will be the one that delivers hope. There are people that you will meet that need you to take control of the wheel of your life and drive down the right path. Stop where you are and make the determination that you can change your landscape.

When an artist is painting an oil painting there are a few steps that have to be taken to prepare the canvas. You can't paint a masterpiece on untreated cloth. Raw canvas is rough and can't be painted on. The primer fills in all of the imperfections and smoothes out the surface so that the fine oils can be laid down. If a painter isn't happy with the painting he has the option of starting over. He can lay down more primer and start with a clean canvas.

You are the painter. If you don't like the landscape that you've painted then take control. Find out where the imperfections lie and smooth them out. You have the ability to right wrongs by taking the action steps that we outlined in the previous chapters.

ACCOUNTABILITY

The best way to change and to help others change is to be accountable to yourself. Keeping a record of your goals by dating them and taking action steps will help you to improve your accountability.

Imagine that you were a teacher in the second story about Rachel. What do you think your students would think of you if they knew that you treated another teacher badly? Do you think that you would garner their respect? If the principal had made you accountable for your actions would you have treated Rachel differently?

Mature and emotionally intelligent people hold themselves accountable for their actions. If you require some one to hold you accountable for your actions then you haven't taken the time to understand who you are. You can only be effectual when you have a clear knowledge of your sense of right and wrong.

Today's society calls for us to compromise on many levels of what we hold as true. As a transformational leader your duty to others is to stand firm on your day to day decisions to uphold a moral stance. It is not easy to be accountable to yourself if you can't find balance. That is why it is important to predetermine your course and change your course if you see that you are faltering.

CONCLUSION—BUILDING A CLASSROOM WITH TRUTH

The three things that will impact your leadership the most are reliability, respect and reputation. As a leader your credibility is affected by all three. What you say will have little meaning to others if you have nothing that you can stand on as truth. People will follow leaders that they can trust. We've said that before. People do follow leaders that they can't trust for a time but those leaders readily lose their credibility in the face of opposition. If you can stand for your values you will be effective in leading. That is not to say that everyone will follow you because you are right. It only says that at the end of the day, those that follow you will be made better and more whole if you are honest. Before you are honest to others, be honest to yourself.

Before you try to offer hope to others, offer hope to yourself. Before you declare truth to others, know the truth for yourself.

Here are the three steps that you can take to build purpose in your classroom:

✓ **Step 1:** Remember that reliability, respect, and reputation are the key ingredients in credibility. Write at least two goals for each.

✓ **Step 2:** Teach your students the value of honesty and truthfulness. Offer hope by showing them the importance of being true to themselves.

✓ **Step 3:** Teach them to hold fast to their values and not to compromise.

The river of change is continually flowing. That is a good thing. As you walk in the river and encounter snakes, step aside before they bite you. Take the high ground. Don't dam the waters so that they can't flow. Walk in the clear water and enjoy the view.

5

Reducing the Hate

*Prejudices, it is well known, are most difficult to eradicate from
the heart whose soil has never been loosened or fertilized by
education; they grow there, firm as weeds among rocks.*

~Charlotte Bronte

Hate is always a clash between our spirit and someone else's body.

~Cesare Pavese

STRATEGY: CREATE A GRUDGE-FREE LEARNING ENVIRONMENT

THE GRUDGE

Ken paid careful attention in class. He wrote everything down in a special notebook. Every time someone said something hurtful, Ken did not say a word. He simply wrote it down. It didn't really matter to him what was said, who said it, or why. He simply recorded the hate. Sometimes it was more than just words. He recorded the ugly behavior too. He wasn't sure why he was doing it, and no one paid him the slightest notice. Three months into the school year, Ken had exhausted the pages of his book.

Everyone knows someone with a grudge. If that someone is not you, then more than likely it is someone close to you. You may even have someone like Ken in your class who dutifully records hate-filled words or what they see as bad behavior aimed at them. Grudges are part of life. If it was not for the fact that they get in the way of life, we could leave them alone, content to see them as one of those harmless elements of humanity. In the same way that conflicts and disagreements seem to be part of the human landscapes, we might be tempted to say that in ways that we cannot really understand—grudges help to make the world go around. After all, if virtually everyone holds a grudge at some point over the course of their lifetime, then surely grudges must have their use.

Whether in the classroom or elsewhere in life, grudges demand our attention. They are manifested in gossip, showing off, bullying behavior, seething resentment, physical and emotional violence, and even in graffiti. Try as we may, it is hard to escape the effect of grudges in school. Whether they are deeply held, and become stereotypes and hurtful prejudices, or something simply flirted with to maintain face with the in-crowd, the fact remains that it is difficult to ignore a grudge.

If you have never really given this more than a passing thought, now is probably a good time to think about your own classroom experience. Whether as a student or teacher, can you recall the effect of grudges in your class? You probably had other names for what we call grudges here. Hate, spite, dislike, gossip, prejudice, ill will, and resentment are some of the names you might have used alongside words like prejudice, abuse, and enemy; words that no one really uttered, but which were there, hiding behind more positive words like loyalty, friendship, fun, and success.

Apart from the more obvious examples of bullying behavior and conflicts between different groups of students over such things as music, friendships, academic performance, fashion, language, ethnicity, social class, and gender; grudges, because they were commonplace, are what really dictated the ebb and flow of life both in and out of the classroom. If you think this is an exaggeration think of how grudges, whether expressed or latent, influence student acceptance in the classroom.

Grudges could act as either a gateway or barrier to full classroom or team acceptance. Grudges also help shape and direct the definition of one's identity. We are all familiar with the so-called benign grudges held against others because they are clever or poor at spelling, fashion sense, skin color, "weird" hairdo, weight, family background, or simply because they wear glasses.

STILL BITTER

"How come you never said anything when others called me names?" Someone had convinced Murugan to return to his former high school 10-year reunion party. He hadn't really wanted to go. Now that he was here, everything was coming back to him. He knew he should not have come. He had been surprised to find that Mr DeSouza—the music teacher—was still there. He'd always wanted to play the saxophone. That was the real reason he had joined the band. Mr DeSouza had allowed him to audition and then promptly assigned him to the drums.

He took to the drums but only because he was not given a chance to improve on the saxophone. But the worst part of class was the students who laughed for no reason every time he appeared with his drums. At first, he ignored them. Mr DeSouza did the same. However, the sniggers turned to comments first about his clothes, then his hair, and then the fact that he was a loner whose family had only recently migrated from the South. "Odd ball" became his nickname. The teasing and name-calling would continue throughout class. Sometimes he would lose his beat and Mr DeSouza would eye him suspiciously.

Seeing Mr DeSouza at the reunion brought back some of these memories. The teacher had not changed much. Plucking up courage, Murugan walked over to where Mr DeSouza was standing. The words tumbled out before he really knew what he wanted to say: "How come you never said anything when the other students called me names?" Mr DeSouza blinked. Maybe he was surprised at Murugan's outburst. Maybe he didn't recognize the former drummer who really wanted to play the saxophone. Murugan left the party still bitter after 10 years.

The first thing that strikes us when we think of grudge is how similar the word is to another word, grunge. In fact, a single letter separates the two words. While grunge simply refers to dirt or grime, a grudge is something much deeper. According to the *Random House Unabridged Dictionary* (2006), a grudge is "a feeling of resentment harbored because of some real or fancied wrong." Yet, in many ways, a grudge is like grunge. It can make muddy or soil relationships and leave a residue of dirt or grime on everything. In many ways, the classroom mirrors society. Therefore, it is little surprise to find some of the same characteristics of life present in the classroom. Feelings of ill-will or resentment are as commonplace in school as they are in military or political campaigns. A casual reading of the daily newspaper reveals that grudges range from innocent or pet jealousies over grades, fashion, and friends to bullying, the last of which can have tragic consequences. This encourages us to not be too quick in dismissing acts of bullying or playground squabbling as nothing but child's play. Today's child's play may be tomorrow's grudge.

Returning to the connection between grudge and grunge, most of us expect and demand safe and clean physical environments. Yet pollution is part of our urban and village landscape. Even as we go in search of a pollution-free environment and bemoan the loss of all things pure, we have come to accept some grunge as part of the price we must pay for modernization and development. Dirt is everywhere and some have been persuaded into thinking that one of the required traits for modern living is dealing with grunge. Could grudge-keeping be another uniquely modern human trait, substantially defining who we are as human beings? Perhaps grunge and grudge are simply two metaphors for society.

If we ask politely, most people will readily agree that the world they want to create is built on a bedrock of values and ideals. Except in some warped sense, grunge or grudges are generally absent from any list of principles for an ideal society. The classroom or school in general is little different. Once upon a time, the schoolyard was seen almost as a romantic place; a place where children were free to run and play in reckless abandon, developing essential kinetic and social skills. The same was true of the classroom. Students could safely enter the classroom, where nothing more dangerous than learning occurred. We all know that this is more a statement of hope or myth than reality. Conflicts and quarrels have been part of life and school from the beginning of civilization, and long before that even.

The stereotype of conflicts, grudges and grunge, has come to dominate our views of the classroom and school in general. Media headlines, reports from our own children, or those of others have made us revise our once pure vision of the classroom. However, the fact that grudges have always been part of the school and classroom landscape does not mean we should look the other way, fold our arms, or accept that this is the way things have to be. Is does not translate into ought. Transformational teachers must be willing to challenge the status quo, especially when the withering results of that status quo are measured in reduced lives, emotional turmoil, and broken spirits. Grudges inhibit learning, which when aggregated can do tremendous harm to society. For this reason, grudges and grudge-builders should not be left alone.

While grunge is usually a visual, external sign of deterioration and decay, grudges point inward. This may be one reason why their effects run much deeper. Left unchallenged, bitterness, malice, enmity, and naked hatred can fester, resulting in students and teachers who will boldly declare their loss of faith in schools and the schooling process itself. In this sense, grudges can be monumental obstacles to participation in and improvement of the classroom. We should, therefore, all be interested in the potential long-term effects of deeply held grudges. Human development and participation in society are at stake and both teachers and students have an important role to play in leading change.

STUDENTS BEHAVING BADLY

In the United States, the word "Columbine" has become an almost universal statement for classroom tragedy. In Columbine High School in Littleton, Colorado, two teenage students, Eric Harris and Dylan Klebold, went on a shooting rampage. When it was all over, 12 students and a teacher were dead and four others wounded. Eric Harris and Dylan Klebold committed suicide. Columbine is a tragic example of what can go wrong in a single school. Fortunately, for us it is an extreme example.

However, what happened in one high school in 1999, rarefied and outlandish though it was, holds a variety of grudge lessons. We should not reduce Columbine to a single cause. Many things went wrong. Even now, many years later, some are still asking questions. Grudges may seem an inadequate description of what happened at Columbine and at other school tragedies since, though in many ways it is adequate. Thus, taking a closer look at grudges may help us see how resentment and bitterness can morph into our worst nightmare.

Beginning in grade or primary school, children become aware of the self and begin the process of exploring who it is they are or would like to be. Going in search of identity may seem too creative a term for what children do. Yet, that is precisely what happens as part of the socialization process. In an ideal world, every child would be free to grow and learn in an environment free of intimidation and physical harm.

Reports from the schoolyard, lunchroom, classroom, and the streets tell us that reality is very different even for very young, school age children. While professionals rightly suggest that coping with conflict and even paradox are an important part of the socialization and identity-development process, the rest of us wonder just how much bruising the identity-development can take.

Developing social skills is key to developing healthy relationships, which in turn helps in the development of self. The classroom is one important arena where these essential social skills are acquired. Many parents who send their children off to school are surprised to note changes in their character that seem to rise to the surface almost overnight. In addition to independence, self-will, and challenging behavior can be malevolence, spite, and sometimes bitterness. It is hard at this stage to be too deterministic about behavior. After all, we say children will be children and they are still a long way from adulthood. This is true. It is also true that this could be the thin end of a grudge wedge, which over time might get in the way of positive human development and interfere with the child's natural desire to learn.

We all know that bullies are made rather than born. Or so we like to think. While psychologists and other commentators on early childhood education have a lot to say about bullying, we cannot help but wonder if grudge-building somehow contributes to bully-making. However, bullies are only one, albeit highly disruptive element of behavioral problems, capable of being linked to grudges. At an ordinary inter-personal level, grudges get in the way of friendships. In addition to bullying, one of the more painful illustrations of what grudges can do is in the arena of gossiping. Everyone has a gossip story. In addition, possibly everyone has at one point or another been the victim of gossiping. Apart from the lies that are so often spread via gossip, the tendency for stories to escalate in intensity and for rumor mongers to hide behind a cloak of false anonymity makes it difficult to nip the gossiping bud from the very beginning. What starts out as a simple grudge can spiral out of control, fanned by gossiping tongues and manufactured "evidence."

"Ellen is a witch. Just look at her hair. I bet she thinks up potions in her sleep."
"Praveen's too skinny to be on the football team. He'd be broken in half at the first tackle."
"Craig's a wimp!"
"Sarah's parents still tuck her into bed at night."
"Hey Miguel, how come you're always hungry? I hear your mum buys McDonalds on a lay-away plan!"
"Trudy's a nun. She doesn't even wear lipstick."

Where do harmless jokes end and more serious jibes and hurtful remarks begin? Why can one student live with criticism or seem to shake it off while another finds school a nightmare or living hell? The answers to these questions are complex and rooted in society, family, and individual dispositions. We are all different. We react differently. Students cope in different ways. While one joins a rival clique and retaliates, another retreats becoming more sullen. Another student reports to school officials, while others change schools. How many students (and teachers) are affected over the long-term of their school careers and their lives is hard to say. The answer is probably more than any of us will ever know.

We need to rethink the refrain:

"Sticks and stones may break my bones, but names will never hurt me."

The expression of bravado too often masks a deeper hurt. But who wants to be seen as weak?

Few classrooms are immune from the poison dished up by grudges. The temptation is to leave them alone, especially in a climate where there is already poor classroom discipline. Why bother? We all know how difficult it is to halt idle gossip. Grudges are viewed the same way. Why risk getting involved? In any case how much of what is going on within the individual can we really uncover or cope with in the classroom? Who has time? Does it really matter? So long as the grudges aren't uncorked in the classroom or allowed to spill over into schoolyard battles, who cares? This is the danger or temptation that teachers face.

With so many other priorities in the classroom who can afford to devote time to coping with grudges? With very little time in the school day as it is, and with administration looking for tangible, measurable results that are easily translatable into indicators of performance and achievement, who wants to confront grudges? The answer is we cannot afford to sidestep grudges. As already said, grudges will not go away just because we ignore them. Sadly, they are here to stay.

Scratch the surface of classroom activities and student interaction and, chances are, you will find a grudge lying beneath the surface of underachievement and isolation, apathy and rebellion. It makes sense then not only to rein in the rebel as we said in Chapter 2, but also to keep a watchful eye on grudges that can so easily invade the classroom and compromise learning opportunities for all. In addition to the many other hats teachers wear, maintaining a form of 'grudge patrol' is one overlooked. Of course, many teachers routinely look out for examples of bad behavior and grudges are included in that category. However, grudges are only really confronted after they have risen to the surface, when they have become known. All too often, by this time, the grudge has become more than a localized problem. A petty jealousy, minor schoolyard prank, joke about someone's family, performance, romantic life, wardrobe, or personal hygiene by the time it is noted has hardened into malice or seething hatred.

It is not uncommon for grudge holders to believe they are justified. Rationalizing one's grudge is just one of the many ways we find to hold onto them. Like stereotypes and prejudice, grudges seem to have their use. They allow us to distinguish "Us" from "Them", and to classify in-groups from out-groups. Aside these primary functions of grudge, we also like to believe there is an inherent value in reacting to others' bad behavior by responding in kind or meting out grudge behavior ourselves; "After all you started it first" is a common argument for holding onto one's grudge. Although it is beyond the scope of this book, a whole discussion of groups, gangs, identity, and grudges is being had in schools all across the world. Some of these discussions focus on issues related to personal responsibility, identity formation, popular culture, rebellion, addiction, and family life. Others take a close look at what is happening within our communities. Whatever the issues, the fact remains that schools mirror life.

What is the lesson in all this? It is simple: grudges hurt. Students who are unprepared or who, because of some grudge directed at them, feel somehow belittled or lost are good candidates for failure. More generally, grudges pollute the classroom environment. This is more than a case of kids learning to cope with the diversity of opinions within the classroom, and developing thick skins. Grudges challenge their transformational possibilities. Grudges interfere with the process of transformational teaching. For every argument that someone can come up with regarding the function or value of the grudge in developing emotional fiber and developing a strong sense of identity and Self, there are a dozen counter arguments including the heavy cost in emotional turmoil, absenteeism, poor performance, classroom rebellion, physical violence, sexism, racism, name calling, and suicide to name just a few.

Who can really count the cost of grudge in the classroom? Who can account for its reach beyond the classroom into a miserable school experiences, the community, destroyed lives, lost hopes, and future challenges? There is much more to grudge behavior than any of us may ever really know. But we have to begin somewhere. Only by identifying grudge behavior can we begin thinking about doing something positive about it.

GOING IN SEARCH OF GRUDGE-HARBORING BEHAVIOR

Earlier in this chapter we compared grudge to grunge, saying that grudges are little different from dirt or grime. They get in the way of cleanliness and decency. In some ways, the terms cleanliness and decency are foreign to many school environments. They may well be foreign to many other environments and communities. Yet, we hold onto them as ideals. Dirt and grime get in the way of pollution free or positive environments, so too do grudges interfere with our search for wholesome classroom environments and the universal quest for validation as a human being.

Holding grudges goes against the grain of a positive, values-based, humane classroom environment where individuals and learning are valued and hostile, negative or "trash talk" is exposed for what it is—unhealthy and dangerous. So who are the grudge holders in your classroom? Do you know? How do you identify grudge harboring behavior without labeling students? Perhaps the first thing to accept is that grudges are well established in your classroom. In other words, begin by taking them as real and common. This will alert you to the magnitude of the problem. A solution that only tinkers with grudges is unlikely to have any lasting effect. As long as we keep the scale and spread of the problem in view we have a good chance of coming up with a workable strategy for dealing with it. However, this is only a first step.

Identifying the signs of grudge-harboring behavior is both an art and a science. Searching for the signs of rebelliousness in teens, understanding different tastes in music and dress, observing the physical and emotional changes that students are going through, being sensitive to what may be happening on the domestic front, or making the connection between the home and the classroom, are all well-established "scientific" tools that will help the teacher identify signs of grudge behavior. There are no easy or simple ABC-type solutions. This is probably the second most useful point to note.

Every student is different. As much as we want to classify and categorize students according to their generation, age, musical interest, arts or science, gifted or below average, outspoken or shy, rebellious or obedient, the truth is every category of student comes bearing its own grudges. Being aware of this will help you deal with grudges from what you regard as strange quarters. No one ever told you that students with straight A's were capable of holding grudges too. Well, even if they did, you would never have expected it from Angela who suddenly and without any explanation has been acting up in class and was exposed as the brain behind the poison pen letter that said terrible and hateful things about a fellow student. Angela was as near perfect as any student could be. That is until now.

What went wrong? Could you have been wrong about her all along? In *Nobody Left to Hate: Teaching Compassion after Columbine*, Elliot Aronson (2000) tells us that high schools are hostile places and concludes that steps should be taken to ensure that students become more accepting of each other. This is another reason why we need to keep a lookout for the grudge and not write off any students as having no grudges or, more importantly, being incapable of holding a grudge. The student who is incapable of holding a grudge has not yet been born. Transformational teachers are committed to recognizing the signs of grudge-harboring behavior and increasing the capacity for grudgeless classroom environments. Already more than enough is expected of the teacher in a normal school day. Simply keeping up with the existing roster of duties and working to a set of state, private or other guidelines can be work enough. Besides this, the thought of going on grudge patrol may sound like an invasion of student's natural exuberance and at worst a limiting of their learning potential.

In a sense then grudge patrol is viewed by some as the most natural form of problem-based learning. Any thought of monitoring grudge behavior or attitudes is subsequently linked to the work of thought police; and didn't we oppose that during the Second World War and everywhere since? Being apprehensive or resistant to grudge monitoring makes perfect sense. After all, it runs counter to our sense of decency and democratic idealism, which feeds into a sort of *summum bonum* or highest good. However, identifying the signs of grudge behavior is a necessary precondition to unleashing the potential of transformational teaching. The renewal of hope in the classroom is one of the practical benefits of identifying grudge behavior.

Challenging the hatred that begins with grudges is the best form of sharing and caring. Everyone should be made to recognize that grudge keeping is counterproductive. There are important lessons here for life beyond the classroom. As well as the obvious practical advantages of rethinking the classroom as a place of hope where caring and sharing can thrive, there is also the important call of transformational teaching. The best teachers are not only those who do things right. They are also those who are forever seeking to find new ways to improve on their own as well as on the performance of the students in their charge. The call of transformational teaching is a call to maintain active patrol. The alternative to this is complacency and apathy. The outcome of both is individual student and classroom mediocrity. As well as the value of increased awareness, which comes from increased classroom vigilance, the wise teacher will find opportunities to revaluate the mission and purpose of classroom teaching.

INTERFERING WITH TRANSFORMATION

Treat people as if they were what they ought to be and you help them to become what they are capable of being.

~Goethe

The main message of this chapter is that grudges get in the way of individual human and group transformation. In fact, they do a lot more than just get in the way. They create an almighty chasm between what some students are and what they are capable of becoming; what we otherwise label their potential. Grudges are major interfering mechanisms. Because we can all recall our own grudge moments we tend to see them as natural, as important a part of our classroom legacy as orientation, examination results, sports, our favorite teachers, and cliques. However, we can order our classrooms differently. Transformational classrooms are established on clear principles that demand we address those behaviors and attitudes, which harm or hinder positive change.

Grudges have been getting in the way of transformation for as long as anyone can remember. Every classroom generation has come bearing its grudges. As much as we might like to think it so, there was no Golden Age when grudges did not exist. Bringing them into the foreground allows us to see grudges for what they really are, which is as the chatter and hurt that obscure the real purpose of education. The question arising from this is: How do we create grudge-free classrooms? The simple answer is: one day at a time, with determination and a plan.

GRUDGE-FREE TEACHING AND LEARNING

Have you ever been at sea in dense fog, when it seemed as if a tangible white darkness shut you in and the great ship, tense and anxious, groped her way toward the shore with a plummet and sounding line, and you waited with a beating heart for something to happen? I was like that ship before my education began, only I was without compass or sounding line, and no way of knowing how near the harbor was. Light! Give me light! was the wordless cry of my soul, and the light of love shone on me in that very hour.

(Helen Keller in Quotes.net, 2008)

If you ask them, some students will describe their experience of school as being similar to a dense fog. It is hard to learn anything when you are waiting with a beating heart for something to happen. Until we commit to ridding our classrooms of grudges, it is hard to see how real teaching or learning can begin. This is hard to accept, especially in an imperfect world.

What follows are some general ideas to get started. There is nothing magical about these suggestions, which should not be seen as the only approach possible. The ideas and suggestions given here should be adapted to meet the particular needs of each classroom. Work from the general to the specific. Begin with the end in mind then design your plan or strategies around whatever it is you wish to achieve in your classroom. Choose to work on one or more of the themes outlined below, or come up with your own. The choice is very much yours.

How do you see transformational teaching coming to life in your classroom? What sorts of grudges are evident in your classroom? Are there any special issues or needs that warrant greater attention than others? Can you see the connection between grudges and specific learning objectives? How do other school issues or problems within the community link into reducing grudges or a transformational teaching plan? These are some questions to bear in mind as we begin forming our thoughts.

- Be clear—Develop a Grudge Control Plan: No one has time for fuzzy or unclear objectives. The same is true when it comes to doing something about grudges in the classroom. Decide what it is you want to do. Perhaps come up with your own meaning and examples of grudges. Determine what you would like to see and over what time period. This will impose a logic, order, and discipline on your strategic journey.

- Involve others: Participation is the key word here. Transformation is always about investing in the needs of others. If it is to be successful, the grudge-control plan must involve students, teachers, and many others. As part of involving others, plan your classroom introductions carefully. How will you introduce the topic of grudges? Would it be better to talk about stereotypes, diversity, globalization, values, or the true meaning of community? Whatever the case, make room for others and invite their participation in working toward a shared solution.

Be creative even within the limits established by the curriculum or classroom directives. If in doubt, do not be shy. Ask others, including your colleagues, parents, or students themselves. Be careful not to overplay reliance on one or a small group of students. The last thing you want to happen is for your grudge plan to backfire and produce a completely new set of grudges—directed at you and your plan!

- Think diversity: Partly because so much of our individual identities are bound to our physical and social identities, it makes good sense to recognize the importance of diversity in the classroom. However, avoid making gestures that are purely a token or simply reproduce stereotypes. Think of concrete ways to expand or broaden the meaning of diversity. Apply these expanded definitions to the classroom. Are different grudges tied to different groups, classes, cultures, or religions? Just as different people have different needs, so too can different grudges demand different solutions. No two grudges are the same. A grudge against a student from a humble background or single-parent home is not the same as a grudge against an "overachiever" or student who may be classified as "overweight."

- Celebrate individuality: In our rush to build communities of learning, we sometimes overlook the fact that some students are more individual oriented. Some are more disposed toward being seen as "loners" than others. And this is not necessarily a bad thing. In America, we hear much about society being founded on principles of individualism and the sanctity of individual rights. This is an important feature of many other societies too whose constitutions and legal systems, in one way or another acknowledge the power of the individual. There is therefore a place for the individual within our classroom communities. Identity is a combination of both personal or individual and communal characteristics.

For some students the classroom is the place to explore the boundaries of their identities. This is perhaps why at a certain age, even in schools with restrictive rules, some students will find ways of expressing their individuality through their clothing, hairstyles, and make-up.

These expressions of individuality can begin as early as the child's first introduction to the classroom when she or he may compete with other students for the teacher's attention.

Theories and goals of education don't matter a whit if you don't consider your students to be human beings.
~ Lou Ann Walker

It is a mistake to crush the spirit of independence in a headlong rush to create a socialized community or interpret the classroom as a sort of team. As a teacher, you can help challenge the false association sometimes made between students who simply want to be individuals and non-conformist rebels. So long as the principles, values, and school rules are in place and are regularly monitored for effectiveness, individual personality should be allowed to flourish. Apart from the difficult time some students have combining their real or potential interest in art and science or academic and vocational pursuits there is also the pressure (expressed through grudges) that makes it difficult for students to be both good classroom and social citizens without losing their individual identities. Celebrating the individual may help counter some of the worst forms of sociocentrism or herd behavior that are often associated with name-calling, exclusive cliques, and bullying.

- Be welcoming: Classrooms everywhere are the centers of boredom. This is an unfortunate and unpalatable truth and is not necessarily limited to Western indulgence. Students who have been turned off education may be found everywhere from England and Australia to Singapore and India. It does not help to bemoan the lack of discipline in schools today or replay myths handed down from our grandparents' generation about the way things were. Nor should we suggest somewhat defensively that schools are not places of entertainment. Boring is not the opposite of entertaining. A better word would be "stimulating" or even "exciting."

However, teachers are not wholly to blame. We live in an electronic or digital age. While many schools are still working to catch up with the computer technology of the nineties, students are multi-tasking their way through life with the help of video games, iPods, MP3 players, Facebook, MySpace, blogging, Twitter, and a host of unique social network sites that make it difficult to keep up with the bricks and mortar classroom or chalk and blackboard interaction that remains standard in classrooms all over the world. Even online classrooms have to work doubly hard to distinguish themselves from what is fast becoming a crowded field. Boredom, it seems, is everywhere. How do we resist the urge to embrace it as another one of those developments, which while unfortunate, is nevertheless here to stay?

Boredom will always remain the greatest enemy of school disciplines. If we remember that children are bored, not only when they don't happen to be interested in the subject or when the teacher doesn't make it interesting, but also when certain working conditions are out of focus with their basic needs, then we can realize what a great contributor to discipline problems boredom really is. Research has shown that boredom is closely related to frustration, and that the effect of too much frustration is invariably irritability, withdrawal, rebellious opposition, or aggressive rejection of the whole show. (Redl, 1972)

From a relatively young age, students seem to lose their interest in learning. Some become quite listless, while others become disruptive or drop out of the school system never to return. Educators, parents, and students themselves are concerned. Aside from various factors including biology, gender, family, peer group, medical history, and deviant behavior, all of which feed into student disinterest in education, the potential for something as simple as a welcoming environment to challenge grudges has probably never been fully appreciated. The welcome is an affirmation of hope. It says you are welcome here even if you feel unwelcome elsewhere.

At the elementary level, most schools and teachers recognize the importance of a welcoming environment. Whether in rural Bolivia or urban Chicago, this is evident in the sensory messages communicated in attractive, bright colors, in colorful wall hangings, maps and pictures, and a smiling teacher. As students progress through the grades, there seems to be an unwritten rule that a welcome environment is less important. We say that the need for a welcoming environment never diminishes and perhaps, given the likelihood of grudges developing as one matures, that the welcome increases in importance as the individual progresses through school.

Contrary to what some may say, the "look" of the classroom is important. Even if they do not determine the quality of the learning that takes place, dirt and an unwelcoming physical environment are hardly the companion students need for academic or social success in the classroom. What is true for the home is equally true for the classroom. The smiling, "emotionally connected" teacher is important. Unhappy, surly or mean spirited teachers, however well intentioned, are unlikely to get their message across, or require a much longer time period to connect with their students. This does not mean that teachers and students need be part of the same friendship circle or engage in backslapping exchanges. Neither does it mean that teachers should look the other way when something is obviously wrong, or pander to every student's whim, wish, or desire.

Discipline and respect are the bedrock of good classroom interaction and part of what goes into the creation of a healthy learning environment. Most students if asked will come out on the side of teachers who are fair, knowledgeable, and committed, preferring such teachers to those who are either over-friendly or who believe the best way to win over their students is by being hip, "cool," or building up a knowledge base of the latest jokes.

Coming to class with a positive attitude and outlook, being familiar with the names of your students, resisting stereotypes (sometimes teachers unwittingly contribute to the perpetuation of grudges), learning about the strengths of each student, regularly working these into each teaching day or week, and smiling. These are all relatively inexpensive ways of maintaining a positive outlook and maintaining grudge control.

- Sacrifice or do not look for the reward: This is a difficult one. Doing something for what appears to be nothing, or which has no immediate tangible reward is hard. Yet, this is probably what inspired or transformational teaching is all about. Being willing to go the extra mile for your students is hardly what comes to mind, especially when you are the object of ridicule, negative stereotypes, bad behavior, and student grudges. The thought of doing more for students than required under the terms of your contract is probably anathema to you, especially if you believe you are underpaid. Moreover, in an age where "working to rule" may be somehow equated with professionalism it is easy to interpret sacrifice as a return to teacher servitude. Nothing could be further from the truth.

The call for sacrifice is really a call for a return to service. The grudges harbored by students can destroy everything the teacher seeks to achieve and that the contract requires (Table 5.1).

Table 5.1: My Beginning Grudge Plan

Key Objective	Focus	Specific Things I Will Do
Be clear	Clarity—understand why	• ... • ... • ...
Involve others	Participation	• ... • ... • ...
Think diversity	Differences	• ... • ... • ...
Celebrate individuality	Uniqueness	• ... • ... • ...
Be welcoming	Connect	• ... • ... • ...
Seek no reward	Commitment (sacrifice)	• ... • ... • ...
		Date:

Source: Authors.

CONCLUSION—BUILDING A GRUDGE-FREE ENVIRONMENT

Grudges clog the arteries of human communication and interfere with the nurturing of relationships. Left unattended today's simple grudge may metastasize into something far worse—hatred. It makes sense then to tackle the problem early.

CLARITY
How intentional are you? What do you really want to achieve?

PARTICIPATION
How often do you join with others?

DIVERSITY
Do you honor the presence and contributions of others?

THE POWER OF "I"
Is there a place for individuality?

A WELCOMING ENVIRONMENT
Am I attuned to the needs of a creative classroom environment?

SACRIFICE
What's in it for me?

✓ **Step 1:** Clarity—In a way, the first step is to some extent obvious. What use is anything we say if other's aren't made aware? For this reason it is important to declare your intentions up front. Write them down and if it is appropriate share them with your class and others you hope to influence.

✓ **Step 2:** Participation—Creating a participatory classroom environment helps this process. Most people feel better about situations over which they have some say, even if this does not always translate into control or power. The idea is to encourage a sense of involvement or collaboration. Joint ownership of the classroom is not as foreign a concept as might first appear. Involving others is part of seeing the classroom as a community that we build together. Grudges are everyone's concern. What can we collectively do to be rid of them?

✓ **Step 3:** Diversity—Society is built on the diverse contributions of many different cultures, ethnicities, and communities, each with its own unique experiences, narratives, talents, and contributions to make both in as well as outside the classroom. The more ways we can find to express our differences the more we begin to identify the things we share in common. Improving the opportunities for sharing and learning about others pushes us to devise inventive ways of combating classroom grudges.

✓ **Step 4:** Recognizing me—The Power of "I": Not everyone wants to belong to a social group, whether this social group is classified as a team, club, gang, clique, or simply an in-group. Individuals who resist the "group think" inherent in many classroom activities and associations should not be automatically dismissed as strange, anti-social, or worse. Strange as it may seem, classrooms like society can benefit from the input of critical thinkers who challenge established conventions and in the process introduce new ideas into the system.

✓ **Step 5:** A welcoming environment—Creating a welcoming environment can achieve what hours of one-on-one counseling, academic tutoring, and a physical remodeling of schools combined cannot. Making the emotional connection between the student, the teacher, and other students helps to establish the classroom as a circle of inclusion. This contributes to building the participatory environment spoken of earlier. A welcoming environment includes paying attention to physical as well as emotional elements. In addition to the architecture or physical space, a lot can be done in the realm of emotions and the creation of a social environment conducive to learning and human growth.

✓ **Step 6:** Sacrifice—Sacrifice in this case simply means a willingness to stay the course, to commit to the goal; it means developing a strategic agenda, going beyond the call of duty, and daring to dream with your students every day. The fact that you are not consciously seeking a reward does not mean you will not receive one. The rewards of transformational leadership are abundant and delivered every day in transformed lives and heart-warming success stories.

Before moving to the next chapter, review each idea shown in Table 5.1. Jot down specific things you will commit to doing. There is no right or wrong answer and no need to race through the template filling all the empty boxes in a single effort. Feel free to come back to review, change or add to your unfolding grudge plan.

6

Bedrock or Quicksand

He who has not first laid his foundations may be able with great ability to lay them afterwards, but they will be laid with trouble to the architect and danger to the building.
~ Niccolo Machiavelli, *The Prince*

STRATEGY: LAY A STRONG FOUNDATION

COMMITMENTS

The Great Wall of China stretches over 4,000 miles across Northern China. Apparently, the Wall is the only human structure that can be seen with the naked eye from space. Most people are amazed to know that parts of the Wall are over 2000 years old. Even more amazing are the stories of how the Wall was built using conscripted labor. According to legend, millions of workers died for the cause of this massive building project and some of their bodies are reputed to be buried in the foundations of the Wall.

Today there are more causes in the world than most of us have time to commit. Deciding which things are important enough to commit our limited time or energy has always been a major problem. While some say that today people in most countries around the world have more leisure time than their grandparents, we are also bombarded with choice. Choosing between a vast array of personal or communal projects keeps us busy. Prioritizing the time we spend with our families, friends or even alone is part of what makes us human. Priorities and commitments go together. The Great Wall of China was an immense building project that could not have succeeded without the dedication of millions of workers. The legend of the bodies buried in the foundation of the Walls, adding to its thickness, is a powerful story. How far should commitment go?

Commitment is an important part of success. The greater the commitment the more likely it is that success will follow. In many ways, building a transformational classroom is similar to a major building project. Without a high level of commitment, the chances of failing are great. While commitment does not guarantee an easy process or automatic pass, without it effort is nothing more than a meaningless experiment. Human success is typically built around a formula that includes ingredients like dedication, skill, understanding, and faith. However, without commitment, none of these can really come alive. Commitment is the first rallying cry. Are you committed enough? This is the practical question. How can we build lasting commitment into the classroom culture? Clearly, we have to because anything less than a lasting commitment will not do.

DEFINING THE OBJECT

The indispensable first step to getting the things you want out of life is this: Decide what you want.

~ Ben Stein

Before we can commit, we must have something to which we can and are willing to commit. Put simply, there has to be some clear objective or image in mind. When someone asks about your commitment, they usually want to know the object of your commitment. In love, the object may be a spouse, a boyfriend or girlfriend. In sports, the object may be to win the game or reach the finals while in business the focus may be increased profits or improved organizational performance. Keeping the object or end in view helps to give commitment a real face. Building a transformational classroom is as grand an objective as any. However, is it specific enough? What do we really mean when we say we want to create transformational classrooms? What commitments are we seeking?

Classrooms are made up of:

Physical Spaces + Curriculum + People

Defining the object of your commitment is directed at one or more of these elements. A holistic commitment says the object includes all three components. Building a transformational classroom culture would therefore require attention to the physical space and curriculum as well as to teachers and students. What aspects of the classroom are you most interested in? Where will you focus? What do you want to push? What is your commitment agenda? Defining your object in clear and specific terms will keep you from becoming distracted or lost in a maze that leads nowhere.

ASKING IMPORTANT QUESTIONS

Once the object is clear, you can proceed to defining the issue or problem. The best commitments are not only directed at a specific goal, they are also framed in a way that makes sense. How many times have you opened the door to people in your community or neighborhood who were collecting money for one cause or another? How many times have you been uncertain about the cause or project? Maybe you contributed out of a sense of guilt or genuine compassion. On the other hand, maybe you just wanted to get rid of the collector. Wouldn't it be better to know a bit more about the cause or agency collecting money? What is the real need? The collector and potential donor would both be much better off. In the Introduction, we defined the classroom as the second most powerful space on earth after the family or home. Simply diving into this space without a clear sense of what we are looking for or why we are even looking does not help. Do not waste time analyzing and studying the problem. However, neither should time be wasted getting stuck into a problem that has only been half formulated. Understanding the question makes it easier to define your commitment. How many of the following questions can you answer (Table 6.1)?

Table 6.1: Key Questions

What does transformation mean to me personally?	What goals do I have for (*a*) myself, (*b*) my students?
What do I understand by the word "transformation?"	What is the purpose or objective of education?
	Does transformation really work? How?
Do I have a transformational plan for my class? What is it?	Why am I interested in building a transformational classroom?
How committed am I to bringing about change in my classroom?	Am I generally consistent?
How do I define "commitment?"	
What specific changes would I like to see in the classroom?	Do I organize my life according to a clear set of values? What are they?
Do I see teaching as a career or a vocation?	My main values are:
	————
	————
	————
	Can I justify the above values?
What is my philosophy of teaching?	How many of the values listed above are negotiable?
How important are values to teaching?	What qualities do I bring to the classroom?
How can I instill values into the classroom?	Can I list three reasons why students should respect me?

Source: Authors.

Asking the right questions helps to guide the process of change. Discovering answers to the questions posed above uncovers new possibilities.

CONSISTENCY

A good way to build lasting commitment into your classroom is to be clear about the problem. One reason why leaders are accused of inconsistency is they have not taken the time to think through their questions. Answers become lost in a shuffle from one unrelated point to another. Instead of bedrock values or a strong foundation, we find leaders wavering. Laying a strong foundation demands not just commitment but consistency. The two are connected. Commitment brings clarity (of purpose) which helps promote a climate of Consistency.

Commitment + Clarity = Consistency

Creating a positive classroom culture has to be more than developing a model for today that becomes obsolete tomorrow. Strong foundations take effort to build. Remembering the story of how the Great Wall of China was built is a reminder of the commitment that is often required in life. In everyday conversation, we refer to "digging deep" in our hearts or minds. This is in some ways connected to a search for the deep purpose or reason behind our actions. It could also point to core values or fundamental principles that sum up who we are. The deeper we dig, the surer our foundation.

COMMUNICATION

Commitment, Clarity, and Consistency work together. We can add another "C" word to the mix. This is Communication.

Commitment, Clarity, Consistency + Communication

Leadership is often described as a relationship. Simply put, leadership is a conversation or exchange between leaders and their followers. Communication is an essential component of all relationships. In fact without communication the relationship dies. Communication is, therefore, the glue or cement that holds the various parts of the classroom together. Whether we are thinking about the physical classroom, the curriculum, students, teachers or administrators, communication is what brings these elements together (Figure 6.1).

One of the reasons for establishing a strong foundation is to develop honest communication. Honest communication involves more than not telling lies; it also emphasizes the importance of telling the truth, and of transparency, empathy, and honest motives. Leaders who communicate honesty cultivate integrity. In a transformational classroom, it is impossible to exclude any one of the key elements—commitment, consistency, communication, and honesty.

Another stone needed to lay a strong foundation is "values." Values are what give real meaning to commitments. Returning to the central idea of Value Mining, values are what separate the ordinary from the extraordinary classroom. Values are reflected in the way teachers, students, and others communicate. Speech and actions are shaped by core values (Figure 6.2).

Figure 6.1: **Communication: The Interlocking Mechanism in the Classroom**

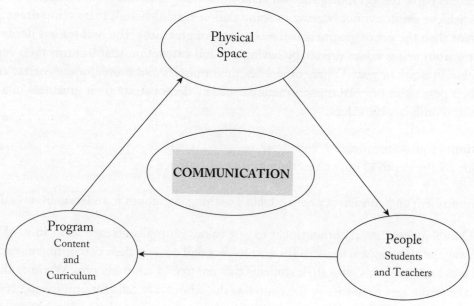

Source: Authors.

Figure 6.2: **Values: The Mediator of Effective Classroom Communication**

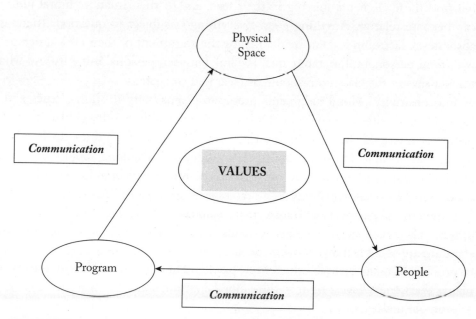

Source: Authors.

One of the most effective ways of laying a strong foundation in the classroom is to stand for something. People respect individuals who take a stand for something worthwhile. Most great leaders achieve greatness not because of some skill or feat, although that is important. More important than the act of greatness is the character of greatness. The best leaders derive their greatness from being values driven, by having a moral conviction that informs their sense of dedication to a task or goal. Where others flex their muscles and minds, or mesmerize crowds with their persuasive oratory, transformational leaders demonstrate their greatness in a commitment to unshakeable values.

Question: How do we measure greatness?
Answer: By the depth of our value commitment, of course.

Commitment and consistency help establish a strong classroom foundation in several ways:

- Moral judgments: A commitment to core values is usually an early indication of which way the classroom is headed. The best leaders will declare their commitments early and build relationships with their students that are free of contradiction. Working through the challenges that arise in the course of the school day calls for unwavering commitment to core values. Everyone involved in the classroom relationship has to see you as steady, reliable, and dependable. Notions of what is ethical, good, decent, or proper arise from these set principles without which the teacher can be subject to every passing whim and find it impossible to lead. Students too will struggle to make sense of the world that is unfolding around them. They will look for commitment and consistency but find these elements missing in their teachers. In this situation, moral judgments can become relative. Anything goes. Everything is subject to question. There are no absolutes. Classroom leaders are defined by the alignment of their ethical perspectives with their personal value statements. The link between personal integrity and what the teacher says in the classroom should be clear and consistent.

- Moral sensitivity: Moral judgments presuppose sensitivity to moral issues and concerns. How sensitive are you to moral issues? Are you able to offer guidance on what is decent or honorable behavior in the classroom? Where do you draw the line in terms of right and wrong? Do you establish clear guidelines? Thinking about these questions and coming up with answers is important in defining your brand of transformational leadership. However, sensitivity to moral issues means more than simply reflecting on your own moral perspective. Transformational leaders have a responsibility to think of others. This consideration of others extends to moral questions. Awareness and understanding are often lacking in public debates. Insisting on a one-dimensional approach to problem solving exclude others from participating. Moral sensitivity means recognizing that others have a right to their moral commitments. Sensitive teachers are able to promote dialogue.

- Alignment of behaviors and beliefs: Commitment and consistency are expressed in many different ways. Aligning words to actions is an obvious example. In simple terms, character is expressed in the things we say as well as the things we do. When our words match our deeds, then alignment exists. Bringing our lives into alignment is a lifelong task. Most people live inconsistent lives. Some persuade themselves that this is the natural order of things. However, order in the classroom requires teachers to join their beliefs or values to their behaviors. The word we use when this happens is integrity. Integrity in turn evokes terms like honesty, honor, and truth. If values are central to creation of a transformational classroom culture, then integrity is the foundation of that culture. Teachers are called to "walk the talk" of their values. They should say what they mean and mean what they say. This is the only way to develop a transformational culture. Most cultures place a high value on leaders whose words match their deeds. In addition, even though it has become popular for some individuals to draw a line between so-called private and public spheres, transformational leaders recognize that this can create inconsistency. Principles and practice must come together or teachers and their classrooms will be forever separated.

THE LEADERSHIP OF SELF—LEADING FROM THE INSIDE OUT

Each of us has a fire in our hearts for something. It's our goal in life to find it and to keep it lit.

~ Mary Lou Retton

Everything begins with you. Whether in or out of the classroom the starting point of the transformational journey is self. Commitment and consistency are obviously associated with self. Values, beliefs, words, actions are all expressed individually. This is why self-discipline is so important. How can you lead others if you have not worked out how to lead yourself? This is obviously part of the call for consistency and alignment. In this case, we must first demonstrate that we ourselves are disciplined before we can make the same demand of others.

"Set your own house in order first" is an appropriate aphorism. The ego is a powerful tool and has probably been the cause of many failed leadership adventures. Developing a strong sense of self includes the development of individual personality and character. Leading oneself may seem natural. We all think we know what is best for us. However, many self-development plans end badly because the individual made a wrong start. Transformational teachers cannot afford to stand outside their classrooms muttering about their personality, self-image, or self worth. In this case, too much thinking is not helpful and can produce the shifting or sinking sands that threaten classroom stability.

These days self-help books are more popular than ever. Everyone has become an expert on how to remake or even remodel the individual personality. Every bookstore and library has a section or several sections dedicated to helping individuals connect with their real selves or to boost their self-image. In addition, the Internet has spawned countless websites on the same subject. It is now possible to take a variety of different personality tests online and have them scored almost immediately. Self Help and Self-worth are a cottage industry and talk shows have latched onto the phenomenon. We all surf the net, tune in to our favorite TV talk show, and browse the Self-Help sections of bookstores more than we did even a decade ago. Yet what are we to do with all the knowledge that is now available literally at our fingertips? Most of us are unsure. One of the demands of a teacher is to develop a clear sense of sense and what one has to offer. Confidence should not be equated with arrogance. Two good tips for leadership and self-development are:

1. Positive self-talk: This is a good way of overcoming the doubt that often creeps into our conversations with self. However, it is not good to squash the doubts completely. Challenging who we are can be a good way of making improvements to our lives. It is also part of what is required to develop a spirit of humility. Having said this, the power of positive thinking remains a powerful tool. The message is simple: expect the best from yourself.

2. Positive reinforcement: Managing self by setting up positive reinforcement tools-habits that lead to success should form part of every teacher's toolkit. Examples of positive reinforcement tools are:

   - Think holistically: Explore actions that lead to cultivation of a healthy mind and body
   - Assess work-life balance: How much time and energy are you devoting to these different realms of your life?
   - Action Planning: Balancing life through action planning. (Using SWOT to develop work and leisure routines)
   - Action Steps: Recognize that personal analysis and a program of action steps increase your ability to seize opportunities. Without a plan, opportunities can be lost.
   - Build confidence: Developing a healthy self concept that promotes self confidence
   - Exercise self-control: Curb your appetite. This is also means accepting that you cannot do everything.
   - Think of others first: Support and serve others. Develop an outward rather than an inward self-serving focus.

Working on the self is important. Too many would-be leaders enter the classroom unprepared then wonder why they fail. Unless you are committed to working on yourself, you cannot capitalize on your talents and skills. This is because transformational teachers strive to be their best. They lead with purpose and question themselves. Questions call for answers. Until you are prepared to be remade, your leadership will be less than inspiring.

The most transformational leaders are therefore those who are working on themselves, who believe in the value of continuous self-learning. Many parents who return to school are surprised to discover that their capacity for influence increases.

By working on themselves, they increase their ability to work with their children and others. The same is true of the classroom. The teacher's physical and emotional health is vital to success. Before you can work on building a transformational classroom, you must get the foundation of yourself in place.

SETTING GOALS

If you have a purpose in which you can believe, there's no end to the amount of things you can accomplish.

~ Marian Anderson

Commitment and Consistency are the foundation stones upon which we hope to build our transformational classrooms. Both of these are shaped by how we Communicate and the Values we embrace. The commitment we make to self-improvement also affects the foundation. Once commitment, consistency, communication, values, and self are in place we are ready to begin the journey. All that remains is to set our course or direction. This is where goal-setting comes in. Whether you refer to goals loosely as targets and objects or even aspirations, they are essential.

Few things that happen in life are random acts. Order and design are important. Planning and purpose do not mean flexibility or spontaneity is irrelevant. We need these too. Nevertheless, without a game plan, transformational leadership is nothing more than a declaration of good intentions. Goals help translate these good intentions into something concrete. They are the structural supports for our good intentions (Table 6.2).

Begin developing your goals by:

- Defining the objective: Where do you want to go?
- Clarifying its meaning: Why is the objective important to you or others?
- Timespan: Over what time period do you expect to achieve your goals?
- Identifying your strategies: How will you get there? What specific steps will you take?
- Measuring progress: How will you and others measure your progress?
- Reviewing: Be sure to have a plan for monitoring and evaluating your goals.

From broad outlines, we should move to the more specific. The most effective goals are:

- Specific—Vague generalized goals are unworkable. To be effective your goals should be as specific as possible. What do you want to achieve as a transformational leader? What concrete proposals do you have for your classroom? The more specific your goals the easier it will be to visualize and achieve them. If your plan is to increase the reading ability of your class or improve general discipline, spend some time saying what you mean by these general goals. If transformation is a journey what is your specific destination?
- Measurable—A good way to make sure that your goals are not simply dreams is to be specific and say how you intend to measure them. The chances are that if you fail to measure your goals they will likely not be achieved. We tend to value the things we measure. Measures can be both qualitative and quantitative. Observed behaviors,

Table 6.2: Developing My Goals

Key Step	Key Question	My Response
1. Define	Where am I going?	State what you hope to achieve or where you expect the results of this goal plan to be found.
	Is my destination clear?	Yes or No. (If your response is No, maybe you need to reformulate your plans, spend some more time thinking through your commitments, work on developing your values statements, or on self-improvement techniques.
2. Clarify	Why are these goals important to me?	These goals are important to me for these reasons:
	Why are these goals important to others?	These goals are important to others for these reasons:
3. Time period	What period do my goals cover?	The time frame of my goals is:
	Are my goals long, short or medium term?	Specify one and say how.
4. Strategies	What specific strategies will I use to achieve my goals? What steps will I take to get from today to tomorrow?	List your strategies. These might include, SWOT analysis, cultural awareness, positive re-enforcement, curriculum redesign, personal development, training, etc.
5. Measures	How will I measure success?	I will measure my success in the following way(s): Feel free to combine quantitative and qualitative measures.
	How will I know if I am making progress?	My specific measures of progress are:
6. Review	How effective is my plan?	My plan is effective for these reasons:
	What do I need to change?	Things that I need to change include the following:
	How can my goals be improved?	My goals can be improved in the following ways: 1. _____ 2. _____ 3. _____

Source: Authors.

improved test scores, classroom deportment, and emotional well-being are all useful measures of success. There is nothing more satisfying than being able to check off individual items on a transformational list. This is an effective way of underlining the hard reality of achievements in the classroom.

- Achievable—This is another way of saying that goals should be grounded. We all have flights of fancy when we envisage goals for others or ourselves that we know deep down are not achievable. Sometimes these goals are the triumph of hope over good sense. Transformational leadership theory draws from motivational theory. Motivating your classroom to achieve the seemingly unachievable may seem like a worthwhile goal. And it can be. Everything depends on how you define achievable. The important thing is to be honest. Looking at the circumstances, available resources, time frame, and of course official policies and procedures, how much of your plan or specified goals are really achievable? Remember, honesty is the best policy. Committing to an unachievable goal is the quickest way to derail your transformational train. It is also terribly frustrating.

- Realistic—At first glance, realistic seems to mirror achievable above. The two are related. Achievability has to do with the attainment of your goals. Realistic goals go beyond this and ask if you are able to achieve the level of change reflected in the specified goals. This is why it is important that your goals are as specific as possible. Do not just say for example, "Arun should be more comfortable with Geography" or "There should be fewer disciplinary problems." Instead, say, "Arun should be able to name three capital cities in South America and move from a C+ to an A grade" or "There will be a 50 percent reduction in complaints of bullying." The next step is to ask if these targets or specified goals are realistic. The complaint many of us make is that we have too little control over goal-setting and often live with unrealistic goals set by others. Sometimes this is true. However, when given the opportunity to set goals for yourself, are they any more realistic? Transformational teaching is not like the story of Jack and the Beanstalk. There are no magic beans. Commitment, consistency, and realistic goals are what you have to work with. Cultivate them well.

- True to your values and principles—This part of goal-setting is too often ignored. It takes us back to the importance of integrity and the need to align behaviors with values. It is hard to commit to goals we do not "feel" or which do not spring from our values portfolio. Motivational theory is clear on this. Cognitive dissonance occurs when beliefs and behaviors conflict. Goals that derive from our own clear set of values are much easier to commit to than those that do not. When setting goals it therefore makes sense to propose goals that are linked to your principles, which you are happy to live by. This is part of the consistency principle. For example, if commitment to others or servant leadership is not part of your beginning values statement then developing goals in which service or the consideration of others features prominently may not be true. It might be best first to re-examine your values and then re-formulate your goals.

GOALS AND THE CLASSROOM CULTURE

Goals communicate an intentional strategy. Part of the intentional strategy is to develop critical thinking skills. These skills help to foster a deeper awareness of the environment. The goals set should be environment rich. Are you clear how the goals you propose will help change the environment in which you live and work? This is what the phrase "environment rich goals" means. Tailoring goals specifically linked to the classroom environment helps focus energies on developing a plan addressing the needs of the classroom. At every step of the goal-setting, keep the objectives in view. These should always be related to the particular environments in which you work or hope to work.

Goals are practical schemas that take some of the uncertainty out of the planning process. Until you focus on goal-setting, transformation may simply be a dream. Whichever way you look at it, the classroom is a complex environment and not just for the new student or teacher. Complex environments require a lowering of the anxiety level. Everyone benefits when anxiety is decreased and uncertainties are reduced. Goal-setting is a good way of coping with some of the isolation and alienation which some say is part of the classroom environment. As the self and classroom environment are brought together, anxiety is reduced. The best goals systematically rebuild moral fortitude and emphasize interdependence for the express purpose of enriching and enhancing the classroom journey.

How many times have you heard students and teachers complain about being lost? By lost they mean either that they do not understand specifically what they are being asked to do or feel so detached from the "system" that they see themselves wandering in a wilderness-like environment. Goals help restore a sense of perspective. They also give meaning to the classroom task. If the classroom is initially seen as unfamiliar or even unfriendly, then we can appreciate the benefits of a goal map. Apart from helping you navigate a clear path, the goal map allows you to plot alternative courses, calculate distances, and estimate arrival times. Using a goal map is also useful for making decisions on daily actions. Transformational leaders are specific and intentional about what they want to achieve. They draw up daily action plans (Table 6.3).

Table 6.3: My Daily Action Plan

Date: **Thought for Today:** *A goal is a dream that has an ending.* ~ Duke Ellington **Another word for "Transformation":** Change One thing I will achieve today: _____	**Communicating:** 1. Listen 2. Don't do all the talking 3. Ask students if they have any questions (always wait for response)
Important Scheduled Meetings: Meeting 1 Meeting 2 Meeting 3 **Scheduled Classes:** Class 1 Class 2 Class 3 Class 4 Class 5 Class 6	**Positively Affirming:** 1. Student achievements 2. Community milestones 3. Cultural differences **Reaching Out:** **Contact the Following:** 1. Students _____ 2. Parents _____ 3. Colleagues _____ 4. Others _____

Problem Solving:	Changing:
List existing classroom problems: 1._____ 2._____ 3._____ The problem I will focus on today: Goal: _____ Step 1 Step 2 Step 3	The One change I expect to see today: Change: _____ What the change means?: Meaning:
Creating: New ideas for transformational teaching: 1. 2. 3.	Notes:

Source: Authors.

Ensuring that the goals you set are achievable is important. However, you should also recognize that difficult goals can lead to higher performance as individuals reach higher than they originally thought possible. This is what transformational leadership strives to achieve. They motivate or encourage their followers to reach for a vision of higher performance for the greater good of others. Sports coaches, military commanders, spiritual advisors, counselors, teachers and others working to bring forth the best in others are all in the transformational business.

The reason most people never reach their goals is that they don't 'define' them, or ever seriously consider them as believable or achievable. Winners can tell you where they are going, what they plan to do along the way, and who will be sharing the adventure with them.

~Denis Watley

Goals serve as a rallying point and evoke commitment to a vision or purpose. In Canada, most high school students know about Terry Fox, whose vision led him to complete 3,339 miles of a grueling cross-Canada run for cancer research. In the United States, many continue to be inspired by the rallying cry of Martin Luther King Jr's, "I Have A Dream" speech delivered in August 1963 at the Lincoln Memorial in Washington, D.C. In many ways the visions of Terry Fox and Martin Luther King Jr, struck a national chord and helped bring about important changes in society. Transformation is fundamentally about change. Goals are also about change. The goals we set are calculated to take us from one place to another. Goals stimulate change and are a motivator for future hope. Teachers with positive goals inspire change in their students.

CONCLUSION—BUILDING A CLASSROOM WITH PURPOSE

When leaders build a vision for the class in terms of long-term goals and accomplishments they give students an insight into the benefits of scenario planning for their own lives. Thinking beyond today is important not only from a careers point of view. Students who plan are more likely to succeed simply because they are conscious about their futures.

Planning is an excellent way of reducing the tensions and anxieties brought on by living in an uncertain world. Planning does not mean all circumstances become predictable. That would take the fun and creativity out of life. However, whether you see yourself as a left or right brain person planning increases awareness of skills and strengths, and heightens the ability to take advantage of opportunities. Having a game plan means there is no excuse for walking through life blindly. Transformational leaders prepare for tomorrow, today. They provide their students with detailed support and feedback about goals accomplished. This communicates the value of coaching and mentoring to the learning process.

Encourage students to work on their life plans. Do not wait until students begin asking questions about their career or future prospects. The sooner you begin; the sooner students will appreciate the benefits of preparation. Encouraging projects such as autobiographical essays and genograms[1] help individuals connect not only with who they are, but also to develop their relationships with others. Exploring talents and discussion of moral questions allows students to make connections between values and society. Every attempt to get them thinking and talking about their own value purpose should be encouraged. This is how to build a purposeful classroom—from the ground up! As students are encouraged to plan and to think intentionally, a spirit of earnestness and excellence is cultivated.

Students who are earnest about the classroom and their futures approach both with hope. Commitment and consistency are the natural products of an earnest attitude. Students are often stereotyped as being part of the "now" or "me" generation. Many are denounced for having fallen under the spell of popular, typically, Western culture. Anything we can do to counter this shallow and largely untrue image is worth pursuing. Setting goals can do this. By working on the foundation of your classroom, you can envision the future building that you, working with your students, can bring about. Do you lack motivation? Does the word "commitment" mean very little to you? Set goals for yourself and for your classroom. Before doing this, think of the important ABCs:

---

[1] The genogram is a graphic representation of family members usually over three or more generations. It includes the social, historical, medical, and other relationships between individual members.

ASK questions.
Where are you headed and why?

BELIEVE in what you are doing.
How deep is your commitment?

CLARIFY your values.
Are your principles clear?

- ✓ **Step 1:** Self—After the ABC's comes the hard work. WORK on the foundation called "self." Are you physically and emotionally healthy?
- ✓ **Step 2:** The foundation—You will be amazed at what a little thinking about your foundation can accomplish. Do not worry if your beginning goals are cautious. Even those working on the Great Wall of China had to start somewhere. The more challenging goals will come later. Work on the beginning foundation and lay it well. The strength of your building or classroom will be as strong as your foundation.

The next time someone asks how you and your class are doing, point to your foundation. Show them how solid it is. Share your goals and commitment to a program of lasting change. Tell everyone who will listen; transformation is not a passing phase. It is here to stay. Unlike The Great Wall of China, your classroom may not yet be visible from space. But that does not matter. The strength of your wall is actually the foundation of your classroom.

When was the last time you checked your foundation?

7

What You Say is What You Get

*We know what a person thinks not when
he tells us what he thinks, but by his actions.*

~Isaac Bashevis Singer

STRATEGY: AFFIRMING THROUGH TRANSFORMATIONAL COMMUNICATION

DEFINITION OF TRANSFORMATIONAL COMMUNICATION

Transformational communication is about affirmation. Let's look at the deeper side of affirmation to get a whole view of the vital role it plays in communication. Affirmation is the act of believing and declaring that something is true. It is a positive assertion. Earlier we explored the STRENGTHS section of your SWOT analysis. Strengths are the recognition of positive assertions about oneself. As you assert or believe that something is true you set motion to a belief. In other words, when you believe that a particular strength is present you will take action and make decisions based on what you believe about yourself. The key and operative word here is BELIEVE. The opposite of affirmation is negation. Negation is the act of denying. A more accurate description of negation in terms of communication is to withhold or retract.

Imagine that you love to draw and others tell you that you are an outstanding artist. You look at your work and have a certain standard that you uphold as the ultimate standard for an artist. You compare yourself to great masterpieces and negate, or deny that your work is good. Others continue to encourage you but you believe that your art has no merit. Although others affirm your skill you will not be able to accomplish all that you could if you believed and affirmed your own skills and strengths.

What if you did believe or affirm your own strengths as an artist but others did not. Imagine that you are very skilled and you affirm to yourself that you are pleased with the outcomes of your work. A teacher who is influential in your growth negates your ability to draw. Do you decide in your mind that you do not have the ability and move forward or do you listen to others and believe that you do not?

This example is one of the major dilemmas that people face. Transformational communication can affirm or it can negate. It is serious business either way. How we communicate worth to ourselves and others is a deep responsibility (Muchinsky, 2003: 429). We can in fact destroy some of our own strengths through negative self talk. We can destroy others through convincing them of a negative assumption. When you delve into this type of communication you are really opening yourself up to a denial of worth. We discussed worth in an earlier chapter. You have worth because you were born. Your recognition of worth has a lot to do with the way you communicate your own self-worth and the way you see other's worth. Communication is the side of human existence that has the power to change lives for the better or for worse.

The Strengths section of your SWOT is the section that you acknowledge your worth in a particular area. Take another good look at this section. Have you left anything out? At this point we would like you to add a sub-section to your Strengths section. This section will be called Building Blocks. Building blocks are the areas of life that you would like to improve. This section is important to your leadership because it helps you to recognize areas that are desirable. If you recognize them, write them out and begin to plan goals to achieve them, they will happen. Here is an example to get you started.

Building Blocks

- Listening Skills, June 2008: I want to be known as a good listener. My listening skills will aid my ability to be a better leader. My intention is to do the following:

    1. Listen carefully when my students talk to me. I will listen with my attention to the details that are vital in understanding who they are as a unique individual.
    2. I will take notes on vital facts so that I can review and remember details.

- Positive thoughts, August 2009: I want to improve my thinking by concentrating on positive rather than negative self talk. My intention is to do the following:

    1. I will pay close attention to my speech. When I say negative things I will write them down so that I can monitor how often I reinforce negative actions in my life.
    2. I will purposefully listen to how others use affirmation in their speech and add affirming speech to my own communication.

Leave at least half a page for each new Building Block so that you can follow up with entries. It is important to date your entries so that you can track them and add them to your strengths as you see substantial improvement. You can use your Weakness section as a start for changing your behavior in the right direction.

How does this improve your leadership? It is a roadmap to help you see progress in your life. As you are clear on how to build your own road map, it will be clear how to coach others. Teaching the tools that help people realize goals is a positive transformational process because the path is intentional. Rather than leading others through a "winging it" approach, you are showing them that there is a reason to build a plan. There is a reason to monitor progress and there is a reason to set new goals for successful living.

Circumstances can be seen in a whole different light when you view them in a category. When you can place a circumstance under a strength, weakness, opportunity, threat, building block or goal you will see how it ties in with other significant or insignificant events. Your life will take on new meaning as you realize that the events and circumstances actually are building a beautiful picture of legacy. The next step is to realize that how you communicate the impact of your changes will change the life of others. Communication becomes the force that drives future events.

THE ALTERING EFFECTS OF AFFIRMATION

With every human encounter a reaction occurs. We continually make judgment every time we communicate. Some people have a favorable reaction on people and others have a hard time in their sequence of communication.

In 2006 Mr Phipps taught an Introduction to Business class. There were 38 students in the class and on the first night Mr Phipps asked the students to introduce themselves and say a short sentence about what makes them unique. There was the typical variety of descriptions such as, "I'm Pat, I am unique because I'm a black belt in Tai Kwon Do" and, "Hi, I'm Sam, and I'm unique because I won a contest last year for eating the most hotdogs in a two minute sitting at my fraternity." One of the best responses came from a student named David. "I'm David. I'm unique because I'm the class clown. I've never been in a fight and people think that I'm funny."

The response was outstanding. Everyone in the room laughed out loud. The class really took notice of him. At the break many students crowded around him and a lot of laughing surrounded him as he made his way back to class. Throughout the semester every time David spoke people laughed. He seemed to gather friends like a magnet. There were no shortage of girls for David to talk to and everyone wanted him on their team for group projects.

Mr Phipps became very curious about David's behavior. He was curious because he never really heard David say anything unusual or even remotely funny. In fact, almost everything he said was very commonplace but people had this special reaction. He did notice that David smiled just before he spoke and shifted in his seat as if he was waiting for the positive reaction. David communicated in a way that made everyone listen. Even though David wasn't particularly intelligent, handsome, or witty he had a little something extra that others did not have.

After class one day Mr Phipps asked to speak to David. "I've been observing you this whole semester and I want to know the secret to your communication. You have managed to rally everyone in this class to follow you and yet I don't sense that you are particularly smarter than the other students. In fact, I see many students in this class who surpass your capabilities. Do you know the secret to your success?"

David smiled the entire time Mr Phipps was talking. He wasn't mocking Mr Phipps by any means. He just smiled with a look of satisfaction. "Sure," David said. "I can tell you but you might not believe me."

"Tell me," Mr Phipps prompted. "I would sure love to have the friends you seem to have."

David lowered his voice as if trying to keep anyone from overhearing his secret. "When I was a young boy I moved to a new neighborhood. The kids terrified me. They all seemed to be more athletic, smarter, and tougher than I could ever dream of being. One day when some of the older guys were picking teams for a neighborhood baseball game I could see that I was going to get picked last. I didn't want to be the guy left until the end so I spoke up. Pick me! I yelled. I'm the class clown! I got a great response. Everyone laughed. I didn't say anything particularly funny I just affirmed that I was funny and everyone thought that I was."

David finished and looked at Mr Phipps. He stood totally motionless. Mr Phipps scratched his head.

"So that's your secret?"

"Yep!" David said. "That's it. I used the power of suggestion and everyone ever since that time believes me."

"Do you believe that you're funny?" Mr Phipps asked.

"Not that funny. I think that everyone is waiting for something funny and they just laugh at whatever I say because I make them feel good. I give them what they all want; a little fun. I don't hurt anyone or say anything that's mean. I really just say what comes to mind."

Mr Phipps tilted his head to the side and stared at David. "So what you are saying is that use the power of affirmation to sway people into believing that you are funny and that no one ever fights with you?"

"That's it," David said. "I wish it was more exciting than that but it works and I'm a happy guy."

"I can see that," Mr Phipps agreed. "So you have a profound affect on the lives of people you hardly know by telling them that you are the safe guy. You are the guy to hang around so that you too can feel good."

"You've got it," David agreed. "But, hey, don't tell anyone my secret. I don't want to blow a good thing."

THE SECRET POWER OF AFFIRMATION

Affirmation is really the YES of life. Saying yes to what you wish to affirm is powerful because it tells your mind what direction you want to head. As in the case of David, not only does affirmation help you to say YES, it also helps others around you to say YES to what you affirm and believe.

The secret is out. What we affirm we will put into action (Muchinsky, 2003: 145). This is such an important statement that you should print it out and add it to your SWOT notebook at the top of the page of your Building Blocks section.

"What I Affirm I Put Into Action."

This is the key to transformational communication. If you affirm positive self talk and you firmly believe it, you will yield positive results. If you affirm negative self talk and believe it, you will yield negative results.

This fact holds true for your own life and it will hold true for what you communicate to others. Your demeanor spells out your intent. If you look as if you carry the weight of the world on your shoulders, you are most likely going to carry more weight then you wish you had. It is because of what you communicate to others. It sends a message that others react to.

Look at your list of Strengths. How do you act on each of your strengths? What do you communicate to others that allow them to affirm you in your strengths? Take a hard look at this as this is the point that will help you to affect change almost immediately. Ask yourself the following questions.

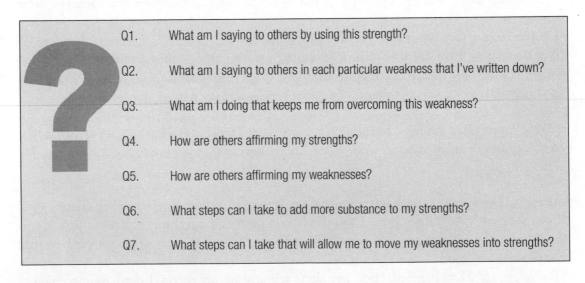

Q1.	What am I saying to others by using this strength?
Q2.	What am I saying to others in each particular weakness that I've written down?
Q3.	What am I doing that keeps me from overcoming this weakness?
Q4.	How are others affirming my strengths?
Q5.	How are others affirming my weaknesses?
Q6.	What steps can I take to add more substance to my strengths?
Q7.	What steps can I take that will allow me to move my weaknesses into strengths?

When you have discovered your personal secret to moving forward you will communicate your confidence powerfully. Affirming your intentions personally will give you a clear direction when circumstances occur that bring about fear or doubt. All that you have to do is look at your affirmations and believe that you have the power to overcome whatever unwanted curve life throws to you.

Think about what David accomplished with his affirmation. He believed that he was less exciting then the other guys in the neighborhood and in one swift move of affirmation he convinced himself that he had the power to be accepted. He believed in his ability to make people laugh and they were drawn to him because he was convinced of his own positive self talk. The key is to move in the direction of your strength and communicate in a way that gives others hope.

THE CONSEQUENCES OF REJECTION—THE SILENT KILLER

In case you are not convinced, you should take a look at the silent killer of all human beings. It is the powers of rejection. This should be explored because transformational communication has a dark side. By recognizing the consequences of communicating rejection you will see that what you communicate has lasting and potent affects.

What is rejection? Here are a few synonyms to help you.

- Deny
- Forsake
- Snub
- Repulse
- Ostracize

- Discard
- Disdain
- Dismiss
- Repel

What you choose to believe about yourself and what you choose to reject alters your character. Let's take a look again at David's story. David rejected the notion that no one would pick him for a neighborhood team. He took an action based on his own concept of his self-worth and communicated his worth in a positive light. What if this story went an entirely different way? Imagine that on that day David's fears got the best of him. If David believed the notion that he was not as athletic or cleaver or as popular as the other boys he would have rejected own worth. His ability to communicate worth would have been altered from that moment on. You can probably imagine that David's popularity would not have grown.

Everyone has weaknesses. Repeat that phrase, "Everyone has Weaknesses."

The difference between the people who communicate positively and the people who communicate negatively is this. People who believe that their weaknesses are profound believe that their worth is diminished by them. The power that self rejection has silently kills a person from the inside out. It has been said that our mind has the power to make or break us. The mind can be altered to understand the basic truth of worth so that positive affirmation can have its affect. Positive results!

Changing the course of the river is as easy as denying the power of self rejection in every form. Denying its power is as easy as identifying its root, writing it down and taking action steps toward changing the outcome.

Rejection is also the silent killer of others. If your intention is to lead by affirmation then you will have to conquer the power of rejection. For some, this is difficult. It is difficult because of many preconceived untruthful ideas. As we explored earlier, we get our values and character from the people that surround us. Listening to negative talk about others and repeating negative talk about others is a form of rejection. Rejection not only negatively affects the person it is directed toward it also negatively affects you. In essence, the rejection of others is the rejection of self because it adds weakness to your character and alters your actions. Here are some results of rejection.

Rejection breeds:

- anger;
- resentment;
- fear;
- malice;
- discontentment;
- a sense of loss;
- depression;
- loneliness;

- physical pain;
- mental pain;
- heartache;
- lowered self-esteem;
- the feeling of worthlessness;
- slander; and
- betrayal.

As you can see from this list, rejection elicits an emotional response. The emotional response communicates negative behavior. Negative behavior alters actions. If you think about the affects that rejection has on a person's life you can see that it is transformational. It is transformation in that it alters the course one takes and this course can bend a life so that it is rendered unfruitful.

ACTIVE LISTENING—MAKING THE DIFFERENCE

As a leader you will decide daily about what you accept and affirm and what you reject and deny. Every action will have a reaction. The reaction that is caused by your behavior can be profound and that is why this chapter is an important part of understanding your values. Your character has an impact on others and it has a lasting effect. Listening is an activity that will help you to discern how you can affirm others (Daft, 2002: 323). Listening is not an easy task. In fact much of what we hear we do not assimilate. What we will propose here is that listening is an activity that is not only done with the ears; it is done with all of the senses.

How do you listen? Answer these questions honestly.

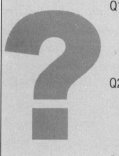

Q1. When I listen to others I am observing their eyes and body movements.
All of the time
Sometimes
Never

Q2. I enjoy gossip.
All of the time
Sometimes
Never

Q3. If others are unhappy with me I internalize it and become confused or angry.
All of the time
Sometimes
Never

Q4. When others are speaking I'm usually thinking about something else.
All of the time
Sometimes
Never

Q5. If someone is distressed I look for ways to comfort them.
All of the time
Sometimes
Never

Q6. I filter what others say through my own values.
All of the time
Sometimes
Never

Q7. I listen to others intently because I honor what they are trying to communicate.
All of the time
Sometimes
Never

Q8. I am an active and reflective listener.
All of the time
Sometimes
Never

Q9. I am a passive listener.
All of the time
Sometimes
Never

Q10. I look for intent as I listen to others.
All of the time
Sometimes
Never

Listening is a form of understanding. Your answers to the questions above should reveal if you value listening as a form of aiding yourself and others. What we internalize affects our output. To be an active listener you must be engaged in a way that answers a few basic questions.

- What is this person trying to communicate?
- What is being said with body language?
- Am I hearing what is being communicated correctly?

As you evaluate what others are communicating you may find something quite different than what is being said verbally. Getting to the bottom of communication is a complex task. Authentic communication is straight forward. Leaders who are adept at interpreting messages see through external communication and seek a deeper level of understanding. Hidden messages are often the messages that are the flags that a person is in distress. By seeking the high road of communication by affirming the strengths of an individual you aid them in seeking solutions to their challenges creatively. The point is that everyone has challenges. If you model confidence in constructing a system of discovery, you will teach followers how to creatively design a path that will lead them to construct a personal value system that will offer long-lasting solutions.

One of the more destructive forms of communication is gossip. Often people feel that gossip is a way to disseminate information that will improve their standing with others. In a high school classroom we asked the students to answer the following questions:

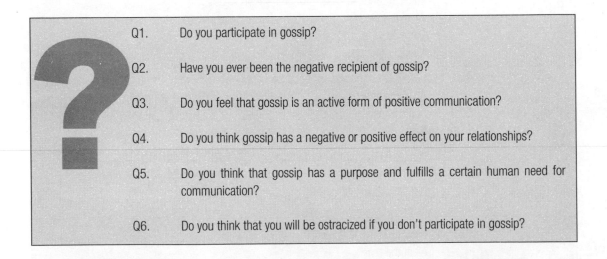

Q1.   Do you participate in gossip?

Q2.   Have you ever been the negative recipient of gossip?

Q3.   Do you feel that gossip is an active form of positive communication?

Q4.   Do you think gossip has a negative or positive effect on your relationships?

Q5.   Do you think that gossip has a purpose and fulfills a certain human need for communication?

Q6.   Do you think that you will be ostracized if you don't participate in gossip?

The results of the questions were astounding. An active discussion produced the following results:

- 100 percent of the students said that they actively participated in gossip.
- 100 percent of the students said that they had felt a negative recipient of gossip.

- 89 percent of the students that gossip were an active form of communication adding that it cemented their relationships.
- 92 percent of the students felt that that gossip had a purpose.
- 98 percent of the students thought they would be ostracized if they didn't participate in gossip.

Do these results surprise you? Although most gossip is the creation and repetition of rumors and has little or no basis in fact, it is still accepted as a viable form of active listening. This destructive activity is one of the silent killers that cause pain and self doubt. Yet, as you undoubtedly know, gossip is prevalent in most societies. Leaders face challenges continually in combating the negative effects of gossip.

Transformational leaders provide vision and model positive behavior to followers. Participation in negative forms of communication deconstructs positive messages. Providing direction to followers and teaching the right form of active listening is a process that requires passion. You can become a passionate leader of transformational communication by following a few simple steps. Adding these goals to your communication style will give you a potent tool to build others.

Communication goals:

- Model superb communication behavior.
- Adapt my communication approach.
- Promoting self-respect.

MODELING SUPERB COMMUNICATION BEHAVIOR

Communication has two basic aspects. There is a sender of a message and there is a receiver of the message. The transformational leader has to be concerned and passionate about both sending the message and aiding the receiver in accepting the message so that both parties have a stake in growth.

Modeling superb communication behavior can be one of the most effective ways of conveying the values of a leader. We will teach you a few simple and effective methods of increasing your competency as a communicator. This, like the other steps you've taken to improve your life message requires you to investigate your strengths and weaknesses. The goals that we would like you discover are a new vision of powerful communication. These goals will maximize your own healthful thinking as well as give hope to others as you add them to your cachet of strengths.

Add this page to your SWOT notebook. Label it: Target Goals for Potent Communication.

- Edify others
- Enlighten others
- Elevate others
- Improve others
- Uplift others

These five simple goals will have a major impact on your interactions. We suggest you commit them to memory.

Edifying Others

Edification is a building process. Building is part of the transformational process. To build is to strengthen. Imagine that you are building a house. When you begin your construction you will need a strong foundation. If your foundation is weak, the house will not stand when winds and other forces of nature occur. It's the same with people. Finding others' strengths and affirming them is a form of edification. Demonstrating how to build on strengths through positive, time-bound goals also aids in the building process. While everyone has weak areas, the edification process seeks to help a follower make progress in moving weak and threatened areas into strengths through goal-setting and maximizing opportunities for improvement. Edifying is affirming another person's strengths.

Enlightening Others

To underscore our point here we will tell you the opposite of enlightenment. Ignorance is the opposite of enlightenment. To enlighten someone is to model and reinforce proper communication. Human beings have a tendency to gravitate toward negative communication. By opening the door of understanding, you as the leader have an opportunity to help people seek their purpose. Remember what we have discovered about each individual's worth. Enlightening your followers about their specific worth will aid them in discovering their own value system. Transformational leaders take the time to help others discover a productive path in all circumstances. By aiding people in constructing and analyzing their own SWOT you will give them the tools to find affirming answers to their challenges. It isn't giving advice. It is offering a system to let them discover their own solutions. Dwelling on the weaknesses of others underscores your own particular weak areas rather than concentrating on building strengths. The process of building strengths is intentional because they have been identified. Without identifying them, people have a tendency to concentrate on the obviously identified weak areas.

Elevating Others

Transformational leaders love to elevate others to their highest potential. One of the basic facts of human existence is that everyone wants to feel that they are important. Everyone wants to believe that they matter and the things that they do have some meaning. Active listening will help you to elevate others. As you listen to what they are communicating, seek to discover their strengths. Maximize their strengths by affirming that you recognize them and offer creative support in the message they are sending.

Improving Others

What message are you sending when you communicate? Is your speech peppered with uplifting messages? Transformational leaders seek to build (Cummings and Worley, 2005: 390). Everyone that you come in contact with offers an opportunity for expressing hope. If you can think of every individual's worth as you encounter them, you will begin to recognize an opportunity to add a hopeful message. Where do these hopeful messages come from? They come from your identified values. They come from your ability to identify other's unique strengths. As you seek to add to rather than take away from their own self-worth your words will take on a new tone. Try an experiment. For one day, keep a journal of your contacts. Write down the names of everyone that you spoke to. Analyze what you said and in a few short words across from their name, write down the message that you sent. Did what you say improve them and offer hope or did it place doubt or confusion in some way. Here is an example to help you get started.

People that I encountered today:

- Bill (at breakfast). Talked about the mistakes our boss is making.
- Patricia (in a meeting). Talked about our team project. I gossiped about people I didn't want on our team.
- My Mother. Discussed the birthday party coming up. Came up with creative ideas for a surprise. Talked about how mom is a good party planner.

As you detail your encounters for one day, be honest. You will reveal the exact nature of how you communicate. When you see the type of communication that you engage in regularly you will know if you have a weakness that you've cleverly identified or you have a strength that can be maximized.

Use every opportunity to seek to improve others. Help them to feel good about their accomplishments. Offer support by recognizing their creative ability to use their gifts and values to make progress in their lives. As you seek to improve others, you inadvertently will improve yourself.

Uplifting Others

Uplifting others is the selfless act of seeing a need and stepping in to fulfill the need. When you uplift others you are offering hope. You are saying very simply-you matter and I care about your need. There are many ways to uplift others but the most powerful way is to take personal time to share in another person's life. Often the simplest things make the biggest impact. Spending time with someone or offering a lending hand speaks volumes about your values. In your goal section add the names of people that you will uplift in the next month. Write down simple things that you can do that will show them that you recognize them. It does not have to cost a lot of money or take a lot of time. Intentionally writing it down and following up on the act will offer them an opportunity to improve and it will add a strength you your values system.

ADAPTING YOUR APPROACH

Everyone wants to predict outcomes to their circumstances. The fact is most of life is riddled with uncertainty which can lead to anxiety. Think about what circumstance that you are facing right now that is causing a form of anxiety. Are you facing job loss, a financial threat, loss of a relationship, or maybe difficulty in handling your own fears? It is common for people to worry about what they can't see and even further, what they can't control. Our behaviors are affected by our uncertainty. Have you ever noticed that some people are able to handle uncertainty better than others? Are you curious about their secret?

The secret of handling uncertainty is to watch for the door of opportunity. As a leader your primary strength should be the ability to utilize every circumstance to move toward your vision of hope. Adaptation is a strategy. You should see the advantages of using this strategy to help your communication skills.

Before we explore the strategy of adaptation we should look at what adaptation is not. Adapting is not abandoning your values. It is not changing who you are and what you believe to be true. Adapting your approach to others is allowing yourself to remain loyal to the truths that you hold dear while listening intently to the truths another person holds dear.

The strategy of adapting your approach is to understand that each person's unique qualities are given for a unique purpose. That is the first tenet of the strategy. In fact we will label it as the first step in developing your skills as a superb communicator.

The second key element in adapting your approach is to recognize that a transformational leader's goal is not to change people. It is to help them recognize opportunity (Daft, 2002: 148). As a teacher, leader, parent, religious leader, boss, spouse or friend, it is not your duty to mold any other human being into our likeness. Transformational leaders communicate the message that each person will walk a path that is solely special to them. How do you know that? You can be assured of that fact because there is not one of us that are the same. That is the reason that the best thing that you can communicate is your willingness to listen and offer affirmation and hope. This is the third part of adapting your approach. Communicate that you affirm each person as an individual with a special mission in life. Your vision, your purpose is not their vision or purpose. Give everyone the same respect as everyone also plays an important role in your life. They adapt to you. Being flexible is showing that you are willing to listen and that you don't believe that your needs are far above anyone else (Goleman, 2002: 39). This is a truth that will be a secret of success for you as a leader. Adapting your approach means to hold fast to your values while recognizing the values of others. Listen, affirm, and celebrate your differences.

"Adapting Your Approach—Strategy for Communication Success."

- Recognize every person's unique purpose.
- Don't try to change people. Help them to see opportunity.
- Hold on to your values. Respect the values of others.

People don't change because you want them to. People change when they see a better way for their future. The most important thing you can do is to help them see doors of opportunity and affirm their decisions to move in a positive direction.

PROMOTING SELF-RESPECT

Self-respect is loyalty. Loyalty is commitment. Think about it. Who are you committed to? What are you committed to? (Goleman, 2002: 67). First and foremost you should be committed to your purpose in life. In order to understand your purpose you need to know without a doubt that you should respect YOU!

Respect entails a building a person rather than tearing them down. Earlier in this chapter we discussed the building process of affirmation. Self respect is recognizing the importance of the continual building process in your own life (Kouzes and Posner, 2002: 64). That building process should have a strong foundation. The "winging it" approach to life shows a definite lack of loyalty to the number one person who matters first—YOU. This is not to say that you matter than any one else or that you matter more or less than any one else. This is to say that from your point of view, your point of vision and your point of mission; the first person that you need to be loyal to is YOU.

This is why your SWOT analysis is vital to your progress as a human being and as a leader of others. If you cannot lead you, you cannot lead others. This is a shocking statement for many because their leadership is worked out in front of others without a clue of what and why they are leading. They just know that they have certain knowledge that allows them to be selected as a leader of others whether it is in the field of teaching, banking, parenting, medicine, or laborer. The ships captain must understand the needs of the ship and how to navigate it through the waters. If the waters are rough, the captain needs to keep the boat from capsizing. If the waters are calm the captain needs to know how to maintain its course. If the mast is broken the captain must have an alternate plan to save the ship.

In other words, you are the captain. As a respecter of self you must recognize that your loyalty to your ship requires you to maximize your strengths and reduce your weaknesses. When you help others to recognize their need for self loyalty you will give them a gift that lasts. A healthy sense of self respect will help you to take control of your course. As you analyze your values, goals and opportunities you will see that they require you to act consistently to move in the desired direction. When inconsistency strikes balance is lost. Loyalty to self is learning the art of balance (Covey, 2004: 161). It is balancing your own unique attributes with the world in which you find yourself at any given moment. Being true to self will help you to keep balance. You act consistent with what you've charted and look for opportunities to grow and change. Change only the things that will move you in a position of strength. Hold fast to what you know to be true. Teach and affirm others as they seek to find truth in their life.

FOSTERING RELATIONSHIPS

Have you ever had a toxic relationship? A toxic relationship is a relationship between two people that is like a poison. It is a debilitating interaction that occurs when two or more people do not agree on a particular course of actions. Just for a moment we would like you to write down the name of someone with whom this type of relationship has occurred. Don't be alarmed. We are going to show you a few communication techniques that can help you the next time you encounter a toxic relationship.

> Technique #1: Respect yourself.
> Technique #2: Respect others.
> Technique #3: You have nothing to prove. Be loyal to your own path.
> Technique #4: Inwardly affirm your strengths.
> Technique #5: Say less, be loyal to your values.
> Technique #6: Don't try to change others.
> Technique #7: Hear no evil, speak no evil.

These seven techniques are tried and true methods of building healthy relationships. As you model the way for others your primary purpose should be to foster a healthy sense of hopeful behavior (Kouzes and Posner, 2002: 44). People will not react as we wish they would and they are a constant disappointment when we believe that they should fall in line with our view of how things should be. The fact is, because our circumstances are so completely different from everyone else, it is difficult to function if we try to alter other people's behavior to line up with ours.

True transformational leaders recognize the need to aid others by being inwardly strong and emotionally sound. Inward strength and emotional stability foster balance. Relationships are balanced when they foster the strength of others and emotionally support healthy decisions.

Toxic relationships can be cured by observing the seven techniques recommended here. They are the secret to communicating from a position of strength rather than weakness. If you are suffering from a toxic relationship, analyze how it began and be truthful about your role. Discover which technique you violated. It will help you has you teach others to communicate effectively.

There are times when for reasons that we can't understand, others do not respect us. That is not something that we can control. What you can control is your reaction. Your SWOT will serve you as you seek opportunities to affirm yourself and others. Learning from relationships is an opportunity to grow. Recognize their value in your life. Make entries in your SWOT with dates so that you can grow from your abilities to foster healthy relationships as well as your ability to turn toxic situations into opportunities.

CONCLUSION—BUILDING A COMMUNICATING CLASSROOM

What you communicate to yourself is as important as what and how you communicate to others. You have probably heard the saying, what you see is what you get. In leadership, what you say is what you get. Communication is a powerful tool that can be used to build a mightily or it can be a tool that cuts relationships to ribbons.

Here are three tools that you can use in your classroom that will change your student's attitudes.

- ✓ **Step 1:** Teach them to communicate authentically by looking for positive attributes in others.
- ✓ **Step 2:** Teach the negative consequences of gossip.
- ✓ **Step 3:** Teach them to use their SWOT to counteract the negative effects of rejection.

Great fruit can be grown when we take the time to discover how we can adapt our approach by recognizing the needs that surround us. Every day there is an opportunity to build others. Every day there is a reason to celebrate. As a transformational leader seek to understand the purpose that your life has in relationship to others and foster those relationships with an intention to run a worthy race.

8

Wear It on Your Sleeve

Our motive is not to prove our self worth, but to live up to our possibilities.
~Unknown Author

> ## STRATEGY: ESTABLISH YOUR
> ## TRANSFORMATIONAL WORTH

THE POWER OF SELF-WORTH

Transformational leaders are action-oriented. A leader can take action by aiding in the development of followers' self-worth. Recognizing and developing worth is a valuable and potent strategy. The strategy is so powerful that when developed properly, it will not only transform the follower, it will also transform the leader's own self-worth. It is an investment that pays dividends.

Let's take a deeper look at how self-worth is established. There is a subconscious effort that takes place in the brain when it comes to self-worth. Self-worth or self-esteem is the perception of the worth people believe they have. There are two key words in this definition—the first, perception and the second, believe.

A perception is how a person organizes the sensory input and interprets it into experience. In other words, all of the experiences that occur in a person's life are taken into the brain and the brain organizes the experience into thoughts and feelings. There is a continuous process of perception. Perception builds on itself. Our perceptions teach us what we should avoid and what will bring us pleasure.

Our beliefs are habits of the mind. A belief is something that we place our confidence or trust in (Nash, 1992:16). Our beliefs are also a part of our perceptions because they are a continuous, never-ending part of our understanding of the world in which we find ourselves. Our perceptions can become beliefs because the stimulus that makes us feel a certain way repeatedly will cause us to feel either like we have worth or we do not.

When a person's worth is threatened they react subconsciously. The reaction is a self-protective mechanism of the brain just like the fright and flight response. This is one way in which our perception of worth can be diminished. If our brain senses a threat over and over again, it will react. A perception of the situation will be developed and a belief about it will be formed. That is what affects the way we feel about ourselves. We may have a healthy self-worth because our brains sensed a sense of well-being. Or we may have a faulty sense of self-worth because our brains sensed a threat.

The interesting part about self-worth is that it can be changed. It can be changed for the better or even for worse. Our sense of worth is constantly challenged. It is challenged by external forces that want us to believe we are worthless, or it can be challenged by perceptions that do not really exist. Some threats are only imagined, but they are still challenges to the perception and belief of worth.

Self-worth is a constant and never-ending struggle for everyone. This is an important fact because it puts all humans on an equal playing field. If you struggle with your sense of self-worth because of the circumstances that you perceive have hurt you and you take them to heart; you are not alone. You may be at the brink of a transformational discovery.

Perception and belief are the powers of self-worth. I'll say it again in bold print so that you can see it clearly.

"Perception and Belief are the Powers of Self-worth."

Here is an important point that you should know about perception and belief. Pay close attention to the point that I am about to make because it is the point that will turn your own life and will help you to transform the lives of others.

You Have Worth.
Say it slowly so that you will understand the next important point.
I Have Worth.
The next important point:
Your Worth is Not Determined by Your Circumstances.
Say it slowly so that you will understand the next important point.
My Worth is Not Determined by My Circumstances.
The next important point:
You Have Been Given Life–You Have Worth.
Say it slowly so that you will understand the next important point.
I Have Been Given Life–I Have Worth.

A fact is that we all came into this world under different circumstances. None of our circumstances are exactly like anyone else. We are completely and utterly unique in every way. Your finger print is not the same as any one else who existed or exists. Your circumstances form a perception in your mind, but note: The perception can be changed. Your belief can be changed. At some point in your life you may feel that you have great worth. At other points you may feel as if you are not worth anything. They are all perceptions. If you understand the bottom line of your existence, you will understand the main point. Your worth is not determined by your circumstances, your worth is established since your birth. What you do with you life is the point that will allow you to perceive and believe your worth or doubt your worth. But even if what you do causes you to believe that you are worthless or if someone tells you that you are worthless you can go back to what is written here and know that the truth is: You Have Worth. You are Alive and Your Worth is Great. This can be said because of the unique formation that took place in a womb, making you so different from any other human being. Your unique qualities are not better or worse than any one else who was formed. Your unique qualities make you exactly like everyone else. You are on an equal playing field because your unique qualities can be developed and celebrated for what they are—Unique.

The only thing that we can say about another human being is that they too, like you, have a unique purpose. We don't have to be threatened by another person's perceived advantages or feel that we are somehow lofty because of unique formations or circumstances that we find ourselves in—we were all born with the exact same thing in common—we are not like anyone else. We group and categorize ourselves, and that is our perception and belief. But, if we are to believe and perceive the truth, we are to believe and tell ourselves over and over that our circumstances are part of our journey they are not our worth.

If you can grasp the power of the meaning of self-worth you can continually use it to transform your life. As circumstances occur, you can take them for what they are. They are a part of your journey. They don't make you worth more; you already have worth. Circumstances help build your character. If your circumstances have crippled you in any way, you can lay the circumstances to one side and count them as blessings because they are there to teach you something. Learn from them and move forward in your journey. Help others to lay them aside as well and move forward. If you've grown from your circumstances you are in a powerful place to help others realize their worth. We all have the same worth; it is our perception and belief about it that makes the difference.

PERCEPTION VERSUS REALITY

Often, there is a difference between perception and reality. Perception can be altered because it involves all of our senses. We use our perception to develop understanding of circumstances (Kouzes and Posner, 2002: 65). We also use our intuitive processes to make sense of situations, and fill in the gaps when we are confused. Our brains search for ways to understand the stimulus that bombards us daily. The brain is always looking for ways to protect us from threats.

The brain is a highly actively functioning organ that tries continually to process our past and present. It is easy to see that all that the brain takes in is used to form a picture of who we are and how we socially line up with others.

One of the problems between perception and reality is that the brain can interpret stimulus by misreading the cues. Because of the brain's need to protect us, there are assumptions that we make that are not always true. This can affect the way we see ourselves. You probably have heard people say that they have sensitive antennae. That means that they read cues that others may not. When they process the cues, they may look for ways to filter the cues through past experience.

Often, what we believe about ourselves comes from a combination of what others tell us and the circumstances that we find ourselves in. We can become sensitive to each situation that occurs, filtering and drawing conclusions that affect self-esteem.

Anne was an abused child. When she was eight years old her mother abandoned her. Her father, a depressed and abusive man, became her sole parent. For the first 16 years of her life, Anne's father beat her and told her that she was worthless. In her early childhood, Anne was told that the reason her mother left was because Anne was hard to get along with. Her father repeatedly told her that it would have been better if she hadn't been born.

Anne was a withdrawn child who had difficulty relating to others. She appeared shy and was often confused by others' attempts to reach out to her. She had poor grades in school. For the most part, Anne led a secluded life and few people paid attention to her growing need for self-esteem.

Due to the lack of resources, Anne's father considered her a burden. She constantly told herself that no one wanted to be her friend because of her circumstances. She had difficulty relating to boys because she was shy and many children labeled her as "odd" and called her names.

The past became Anne's present as she filtered all new situations through her abuse. There were times throughout Anne's short life that people were kind and took special interest in her. Several teachers in her school got together and planned a birthday party for her. In her mind, Anne could not accept their kind gestures, using her filter to tell herself that it wouldn't last and they just did it because they felt sorry for her.

Anne was in a very precarious position as a human being. She didn't realize her worth because she believed that her worth was tied into what others said and did to her. Her perception turned into a belief system that did not allow her to grow and change. The perception of worthlessness is a debilitating state of mind. For Anne, the pain was great and the discouragement she faced daily was an almost insurmountable impediment to healthy living.

You probably can relate to Anne in some way. You might recognize a time in your life when you were slighted by others or a time when you felt so discouraged that everyday living seemed almost impossible. It is vital to understand that perception leading to false realities has a cure. If one perceives those cues and internalizes the idea of worthlessness, it spirals toward a state of hopelessness. The reality is that no one is worthless and often it takes a person with vision to offer a glimpse of hope. If you can understand the critical need for every person to feel worthy, you are on the road to being an extraordinary transformational leader.

ARTIFICIAL WORTH

The feeling of worth is a critical factor in a human's existence. Think about it. Almost everything that bombards our minds daily has to do with an aspect of worth. We seek to understand our worth since our birth as we struggle for attention from our care-givers. We strive to do well in school to prove our worth. Advertising continually hammers us about our worth to select the right clothes, makeup, sports, food, diet, scents, and even the detergent that we use to wash our clothes. Our religion, culture, social standing, and living conditions cause us to judge ourselves and others. There is a never-ending assault on our psyche to evaluate our worth according to the standards set before us.

All of the standards that we place in front of ourselves to measure our worth affects who we are, how we act, and what we do with our lives. Yet, most of the perceptions that we have of ourselves are based on artificial worth rather than true worth. The truth is that all of the artificial judgment of worth is a trap. It is a trap that is almost impossible to escape from unless you can personally free your mind and understand that your worth is not conditional.

The idea of worth as an unconditional state is revolutionary. Giving yourself permission to experience your worth as being unique allows you to evaluate your decisions more clearly. Instead of accepting the filters that cause you to judge yourself from your circumstances, you can set up a filter of unconditional acceptance of yourself as unique (Covey, 2004: 147). This allows you to develop your own strengths and talents for the simple enjoyment of developing your uniqueness rather than striving to meet an artificial standard.

While artificial standards may be used as an aid, it should be noted that you should place them in a different category. To demonstrate this concept, we will make an addition in your SWOT notebook. Set up a page in your notebook with the label: Artificial Worth. On the left side of the page make a column and label it: How I Judge Myself. Here are some common examples.

How I Judge Myself

- My friends
- My job
- My house

- My car
- My clothes
- My religion

List everything that comes to mind. Keep this list going over several days as you ponder upon this question. If you are like most people, your list will be very long. Don't make any judgment about your thinking at this point. Allow your mind to fully explore all of the ways in which you evaluate yourself. Many of the things that you may place on your list may be painful as you may feel that you don't measure up to others. Write anything and everything down.

On a second column to the left set up a heading: How I Judge Others. Again, write out all of the categories that you judge others. As you go through the next week and encounter others in your every day experience, take note of your reaction to them. Here are some common examples.

How I Judge Others

- Social status
- Money
- Appearance
- Friendliness

- Culture
- Job
- Activities

Again, this list is personal and you should take a hard look at the standard you set to measure another person. Take time to think about your friendships, your family status, your religion, job, school, activities, clothes etc. A true and accurate list will help you gain personal freedom. After you've completed this exercise make a line from the list on the left to the corresponding list on the right. Answer the following questions:

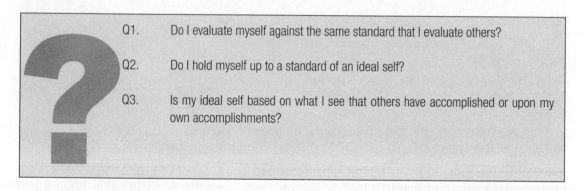

Q1. Do I evaluate myself against the same standard that I evaluate others?

Q2. Do I hold myself up to a standard of an ideal self?

Q3. Is my ideal self based on what I see that others have accomplished or upon my own accomplishments?

Write these three questions in your notebook with your answers. Date them and keep them for further reference.

GETTING TO THE BOTTOM LINE

This exercise should help you reveal a few things about the way you think. If you look at your list, you will realize that you hold yourself up to a strict standard. If you think about it carefully, many of the items on your list will have pain, fear of failure, and the feeling of inadequacy attached. With some of the items you may feel as if you are on top of the world, but very few of the items on your list will make you arrive upon the feeling that you are complete.

The reason for this is that you hold yourself up to an artificial standard that may never be accomplished. The reason that you will never feel a true sense of accomplishment is because we always set the bar higher and higher as we move forward in our journey. Some of you reading this may say, "But isn't it good to raise the bar so that I can meet my goals?" The answer is "Yes." It is always good to set goals and then raise the bar. What is detrimental about this list is the way you have attached your worth and the worth of others in your life. It is judging yourself and setting your values based on what you think others see in you or expect from you. It is also judging others by what you expect from them and believe them to be. You not only categorize others and put them into a box; you also place yourself in a box and hold the lid down. While our brains are wired to sense danger and protect us from threats, we over-evaluate and over-correct so that we can measure against artificial standards. It is the way we view ourselves and others that determines our values.

Now comes the revolutionary part of freeing yourself from doubt and pain. Add another sheet of paper to your notebook and label it: STANDARDS. On the left side of the paper under the heading make a new list of the areas that you would like to evaluate yourself based on your own accomplishments. This is a very important and vital list that will aid you in freeing your mind from the tyranny of loss. Here is an example to start you out. Don't limit your list.

Standards

- Education
- Clothes
- Finances

- Religion
- Appearance

After you've set up your list make a separate page for each item. This will be an ongoing part of your SWOT notebook. In each section, start to jot down goals that you would like to accomplish for each category. You can label the sections on this page as Immediate Goals and Long-term Goals. It is important to write out your goals even if they are in bullet-point form and date them so that you can review them and evaluate your progress. As time goes on, you may find that your original goals were based on things that no longer matter in your life. Turn back to your Strengths section of your SWOT and write down a corresponding strength to each goal. Turn next to your Weaknesses section and write down a corresponding weakness. As you begin to reevaluate your life, you will see that you already have special gifts that match up with your goals. Concentrate on improving these skills and strengths as you move forward. Evaluate the weaknesses you listed and determine if it is a judgment based on your list of How I Judge Myself. Is the weakness based on what you believe others see in you or how you judge others? If it is true weakness and not an artificial one you will have an opportunity to improve. By writing these things out, however briefly, you will become intentional at realizing that you are making great strides toward the values that make you unique and special.

FINDING TRUE WORTH

Understanding yourself is a great gift. It is also a gift that you can give to others. If you can extricate yourself from the tight grasp of evaluating yourself based on others, you will begin to get a glimpse of the great power of your worth. There is power in the concept of self-worth. When you realize that you are free to develop and grow as a totally unique, one-of-a-kind individual, you will no longer have to suffer the pain of artificial inadequacy. Set goals for areas of improvement and measure that improvement in small increments of accomplishment. Each time you conquer an area of improvement, write it down and date it.

As you move forward, you will find this notebook a valuable tool of affirmation. It will prove to you that you have the power to accomplish great things. It will also show you that other people's judgment is not that important to your well-being. Break every goal into small daily affirmations of improvement. If you find yourself slipping into self-doubt, go back to your lists. Add items if necessary. Evaluate and determine if yourself doubt is based on reality or perception. If it is an area that you can change then set goals. If it is an area that you can't control because it comes from the judgment of others, then write it down and move away from it by affirming your own worth based on your own accomplishments, which are based on your special and unique gifts as a human being.

THE HOPE FACTOR

Hope is also a belief. It is a belief that there will be a positive outcome to a circumstance. The direct opposite of hope is fear. Coming face-to-face with your worth will help you and others in your influence to overcome fear. By taking control of your sense of purpose, you can develop a great cache of hope. Transformational leaders are leaders who help followers to see that the journey is worth the steps needed to create valuable and positive change.

As a transformational leader, it is vital to understand the importance of helping others to realize their great worth. When a person is able to recognize their worth and set goals for a fulfilling future, they become motivated. Hope is a primary factor in motivation. Believing that there can be a positive outcome in a circumstance in itself boosts motivation. There is, however, another side of hope, and that is, hope deferred. When the positive outcome does not arrive as expected, it can lead to fear. Fear is an emotion that believes that something is wrong. It can create a feeling of loss. If you are able to diagnose hope you can use it as a powerful tool for change. It can be used to conquer fear.

Consider a young man who is looking for a job. We will call this man Peter. Peter has just graduated from university with a degree in Chemical Engineering. He is bright and has hope for a well-paying job. He does not have any practical experience, although he made good marks in school. He is a motivated individual and his outlook is hopeful. He is excited, full of life, and begins looking for the right position.

Peter learned in school to set goals and high standards. He writes out his goal of finding a job and dates it. He has some resources to help him survive financially for a few months. Peter has friends with connections and he lands several very good interviews. His interviews go well and he believes that it is only a matter of a short time before the right job comes his way and he gets a good offer of employment.

In spite of Peter's good planning and positive outlook, the months of waiting turn into almost a year. He exhausts his resources and must move in with friends. He takes a job as a janitor to help pay for his car and a meager living. Peter begins to wonder if he will find a job and realize his dream. People around Peter start asking him why he is working as a janitor when he has a good degree. They question him continually. Peter's hope has been deferred. This is the point that could bring great discouragement. It is the point when many people become sick with depression. Do you recognize the feeling that Peter may have right now?

Many people will relate to this story. Everyone has been hopeful about a circumstance that didn't work out exactly as they planned. Goals and the best laid plans don't always lead to the outcome that we expect. Expectations should be viewed for what they are—expectations.

Let's take a look at how expectations affect hope. An expectation is something that one thinks is probable. There are rational and irrational expectations. Rational expectations are based on probable assumptions. An example of this is that if there is a heavy black sky and high humidity, one may expect that it might rain. An irrational assumption, for example, might be that if I wear really high-heeled shoes and appear tall, people will think that I could be a good basketball player. If I expected high heels to change my circumstances, then my irrational expectation might lead me to great disappointment.

Basing hope on irrational assumptions or irrational expectations can lead to hope deferred. Perhaps you can think of a time that you had great hope for a positive outcome and nothing happened as per your plan. Think of that situation. Did you base your hope on a rational or irrational expectation? Hope can be deferred either way. Even our rational expectations may not ever be realized for reasons far beyond our control.

While writing goals and working on your personal SWOT analysis, you must realize that your journey may not always have the outcome you expect. There will be an outcome to all circumstances. Every small and large event has an outcome. The factor that shapes the outcome is belief. It is belief that your circumstances are part of the journey and that they do not affect your worth.

The outcome of your circumstances is also based on hope. Hope has true power when it is fluid. What is meant by this is that fluid hope is hope that changes and flows. Like a river, it can move in many directions. It can twist and turn and trickle in different areas. It can be halted in areas and form a larger pool, or it can flow into the ocean and be part of a larger body signifying that it is part of a bigger picture. Just like a river, if you view hope as a fluid and moving you will have an opportunity to see that your journey is part of the goal. The journey of reaching goals is as important as the goal itself. The journey of hope is as important as the expectation. If you are open to changes and movement in your life, you will have the power to experience hope in a life-giving and transformational way.

Your goals and plans should always have the hope factor. Determine that your greatest achievement will be in recognizing that the journey may change your plan. The journey, if seen with eyes of hope, will always recognize that new and exciting opportunities will present themselves. When an opportunity presents itself, write it in the Opportunity section of your personal SWOT. Date it and review it often to see if new goals and plans begin to form. The main point about hope is that it should be viewed as part of the journey and it should build your sense of worth as you see your life unfold in interesting and transformational designs.

THE TRANSFORMING POWER OF AFFIRMATION

Everyone wants to be affirmed. Affirmation is a positive statement to describe something that is desired. What you affirm you believe. Affirmations are so powerful that they will improve your health, confidence, and worth.

When my children were small they were always getting colds. It seemed as if they were always sick. Every time they got a cold I would wipe their little noses and say with a pitiful tone, "You are always getting sick. Why are you always sick?" This went on for many years. As years went by, I started to notice that my daughter would get sick before any major planned event. She got sick before her ballet recital, before her big spelling tests, and before major holidays. In fact the stubborn colds seemed to show up at precisely the wrong time. My husband and I discussed it and decided to try a little experiment. Every time one of the kids would sneeze we would say, "We don't get colds." We said it every time someone said they had any symptom. We stopped saying, "I have a scratchy throat, or my stomach hurts." Instead, we started getting up every day and saying, "I sure feel great." That little line was almost as contagious as the cold. Soon, our whole family said this several times a day.

An interesting thing happened. For the next three years, no one in the family got a cold! We started to eat healthier foods and exercise more because we really did feel great and wanted to feel well all the time. To this day we rarely catch colds. When we are around people with colds we say, "I don't catch colds." The affirmation seems to have boosted our immune systems. We discovered that affirmation is powerful. Try it.

We used another experiment shortly after. It seemed like every time we went to the market we could not find a parking place, and would have to park far away. It wasn't always considered a nuisance but there were those occasions when we had a lot of packages that we grumbled and complained about. One day we decided to say, "We are the kind of people that always get a parking place in the front." It sounds crazy but we had some fun with it to see what would happen. As we approached the store we would start saying our little line and sure enough every time we would seem to come on the perfect parking space. If everyone reading this starts doing it, we are in danger of losing that spot! We were amazed at how often we got the right spot. Why is that?

Affirmation should be short, achievable and measurable. Affirm something positive and do your own experiments. The very exciting thing about affirmation is that it transforms your thinking. When you affirm something, you also affirm a type of attitude in yourself. You tell yourself subconsciously how to function.

Consider my first example of the colds. Every time you sneeze and feel a bit achy you think to yourself, "I'm getting sick." Your mind starts thinking of what it will feel like to be sick at this time. You might even decide that it is a good time to be sick to get out of school or work. You may secretly wish you could lie around in bed for a week. You set the thoughts into motion. You might tell a friend that you are coming down with something to warn them of your impeding hardship. If you get sympathy, you might get the reinforcement that you need to allow your mind to take an illness seriously. Before long you succumb to the feeling and re-affirm it over and over. "I'm sick. I'm sick." The more you affirm it the sicker you become. This is because you have allowed your mind to accept a certain state of being. On the other hand, deciding on a healthy life style and affirming it daily boosted our investment in healthful habits. It is not that you repeat a mantra and it magically happens. The mind is like a sponge that takes in stimulus and puts the body to work to accomplish the task.

Affirmation affects your self-esteem. If you tell yourself that you are worthless, you will feel worthless and you will put your actions into motion to affirm your feeling. You may stop taking care of yourself physically. You may carry a dower look on your face that causes others to reject your company. You will say things that affirm your negative attitude and convince yourself that others don't care. If you accept your worth and reject the notion that you don't have worth, you will subconsciously move toward a steady visualization of healthful living.

Did you ever wonder why some people are able to accomplish great things and others make very little progress in their lives? It is because of the little stories they tell themselves. The brain is like a little tape recorder that records messages and then plays them back.

Set up a page in your SWOT notebook and label it: Affirmations. In a column on that page, make another label called Positive Affirmations. Make another column and label it Negative Affirmations. As you go through your days and listen to the tape in your head that tells you things about yourself, add them to the side that applies. For example, if you are in a habit of telling yourself that you make healthy eating choices, write that in the left column under Positive Affirmations. Date it. Look at your Positive Affirmations continually and make physical and mental notes to yourself to remind your brain to recall these affirmations. On the other hand, the little tape that says things like "you're stupid" or "you're fat" write in the Negative Affirmation column. Date it. The items in your Negative Affirmation side should also be placed on your Weaknesses page. They are areas that you must conquer as you move to a more healthy self-worth lifestyle.

THE ANATOMY OF AFFIRMATION

By now, if you've been following along with these exercises, you have learned the value of realizing your worth. There is an even greater value to understanding your worth than you've explored. The greater value is what you will pass on to others. When you understand your unique worth you will have a healthy leadership quality that is transformational to others. Helping others to see their worth is a great gift that will keep on giving for generations.

The bare bone necessity of understanding worth and affirming it is a vital part of helping others toward a joyful, full life. Harnessing the power of subconscious thought is the first step in visualizing a hopeful future (Sanders, 1998: 92–94). Right now, think of people that you know would benefit from knowing that they are brimming with hopeful potential. Make a list of people that you know are hurting with the pain of the past or are fearful of the future. Make another list of people that lack confidence and would benefit from the freedom of recognizing their unconditional worth.

By each person's name, write down something that you recognize in them as a strength. At this point, many people will struggle. Many have asked, "I can think of a dozen weaknesses." Don't judge or look for flaws. Think of strengths only. Take the list and place the people in categories. Label them friends, co-workers, acquaintances, family, etc. Pick a person from each category and write down a positive affirmation that you use as an encouragement. Think of how you might affirm a special quality or skill. Date it. Review the list often and keep a record of your positive affirmations.

This exercise is going to have two benefits. The first is for you. You will begin to intentionally change the way you think and react to those around you. Instead of looking for a judgmental thought, you are going to seek thoughts that fill your heart with hope. The second benefit is that you are going to help the person with beginning to build their own self-worth. Don't look for artificial compliments such as, "I like your dress, or those are a cool pair of shoes." Your affirmations should be on a real strength, one that shows that you recognize the worth of their character or values. This may take a bit of thought but you will start to see people in a different vein. You will see that artificial worth is empty and leads to the tyranny of self doubt.

To make the point further, try to understand the way that you interact with others. By affirming important and life-giving specific words of encouragement, you will set an action in motion. You will open the door to the person's heart by affirming that you have a real interest in their well-being.

CONCLUSION—BUILDING AN AFFIRMING CLASSROOM

The world we live in is a confusing place. We learn from the time that we are small that our worth is placed on many false external factors. Our true worth is automatic. For some, this is a revolutionary idea. What this says to us is that our circumstances do not dictate our true worth. This is a freeing concept because what it does is allow us to pursue our life with full gusto. We should always have hope because our true affirmation of self should be in the fact that we are growing and changing. Here are three helpful steps to affirm the self-worth of others.

- ✓ **Step 1:** Recognize the values of others.
- ✓ **Step 2:** Tell your students that they have great worth. Confirm their worth publically.
- ✓ **Step 3:** Reach out to students who have lost their way. Help them recognize their own worth by teaching them to list their strengths.

Taking steps toward teaching transformational worth is vital in helping followers grow. You will increase the power of your own values as you recognize your worth. Keeping an accurate account of worth factors in your SWOT will give you the zeal needed to continually move your life in a forward direction. Offer continual hope by demonstrating that you recognize the values of others.

9

The Value of Trust

The highest compact we can make with our fellow is—
Let there be truth between us two forevermore.

~ Ralph Waldo Emerson

The glue that holds all relationships together, including
the relationship between the leader and the led is
trust, and trust is based on integrity.

~ Brian Tracy

STRATEGY: BUILD TRUST

WITHOUT TRUST YOU HAVE NOTHING

Imagine a world without trust. Imagine confusion and conflict or, worse still, no world. It is almost impossible to conceive of life as we know it without trust. When we think of relationships, whether personal or business, we think of trust. In some ways, more than love it is trust that gets people talking to each other, investing their time and commitment in relationships. We trust the people we love and, given time, may even come to love the people we trust. Families, friends, teams, politicians, leaders, and followers all know how important trust is to building relationships.

From the moment we wake up in the morning trust swings into action. We expect when we stand up that the pull of gravity will keep us from floating away into space. We "trust" that our cars, bicycles, and feet will "start" and that the roads or our legs will not collapse under us as we drive, peddle, or walk to work. This kind of basic trust should not be taken for granted. Ask people in earthquake prone zones, or in communities where good roads are rare. But if there is a bad thing about trust, it is probably that we take it for granted. We use the word "trust" to describe our closest relationships and are wary or even suspicious of others. Trust enters everything we do or believe. It is part of our essential DNA. Without some form of trust the world would cease to function.

Yet, as vital as trust is to life it is also something we work on every day. And the daily contemplation of trust keeps us on our toes. The alternative would be complacency. To some extent the quality of our success in life is tied to the quality of our trust. Does this mean there are different types or levels of trust? Possibly so. On one hand, trust is a final uncompromising quality. You either trust or you do not. Trust is an absolute value. However, there are degrees of trustworthiness. The more we know and experience the more mature or "grounded" becomes our trust. This is different from the "blind" or natural trust of an infant for its mother. For most of us trust is a quality we develop over time.

Although there are exceptions to the rule, we tend to trust those whom we know more than we do strangers. We trust the "familiar" more simply because we have had more opportunities to experience their trustworthiness. Most people live their lives somewhere in-between an absolute and relative conception of trust. One is based on principles and driven by such things as faith and hope while the other is based on experience, relationships and hope (Table 9.1).

Table 9.1: Two Views of Trust

ABSOLUTE	RELATIVE
Based on:	Based on:
Principles	Experience
Knowledge	Knowledge
Faith	Affinity (relationship)
Desire (hope)	Desire (wish)

Source: Authors.

IT'S ALL IN THE RELATIONSHIP

Trust and relationships go together. Even though self-trust and self-confidence are important, when we speak about trusting others we do so in the context of relationships. Trust requires communication. Trust connects two or more people. The best teams or organizations are built on trust; when people come together with similar expectations and express confidence in others. I trust you because I have confidence in you. Hopefully, you feel the same way about me. If you do not the trust relationship is usually described as being one-sided.

The development of transformational classrooms has a lot to do with trust. Unless there is a degree of trust in the classroom environment, problems quickly surface between students and their peers, students and teachers, or students and the process of education. In Chapter 6, three key principles were laid out—communication, commitment, and consistency. Trust is an element of communication. Trust qualifies or defines the quality of the communication. Good communication is built on trust while mistrust is often linked to poor communication (Table 9.2).

Table 9.2: Communication and Trust

	Good Communication	Poor Communication
TRUST	Yes	No

Source: Authors.

At an important level, teachers are trust builders. While most people tend to define classroom success in academic or behavioral (example, discipline) terms, trust is perhaps a better measure of success. In fact, academic and behavioral successes are often attributable to this same trust. The greater the trust established between teachers and their students, the greater the success in other more tangible areas.

Transformation is founded on positive communication between teachers and students. Without trust, transformation is little more than an idle promise. Society is littered with the debris of broken promises. The lack of trust at both the interpersonal and institutional level is probably the cause of more broken heartedness in classrooms than anyone can estimate. Restoring trust is therefore akin to restoring hope. In many cases teachers will have to build trust by taking risks and making sacrifices of their time and energy.

Taking risks demands a review of the status quo and commitment to change. In some cases "innovative" change programs demand nothing more than a flexible approach to learning. Creative curricula and improved teaching standards are not always about committing additional material resources. Global comparisons suggest that educational success is often linked to factors other than material investment. Countries with the highest per capita investment in education are not necessarily at the top of the league table when it comes to pupil success in individual subjects, entry to college, or positive attitude. Trust, creativity, innovation, and entrepreneurial approaches to education are all part of what is required for classroom success. In this case flexibility becomes a powerful tool and reflects a teacher's willingness to approach problems with a fresh pair of eyes.

MOTTOS AND VISIONS

E Pluribus Unum ("Out of Many One"—First national motto of the United States, succeeded by "In God We Trust")
Citius, Altius, Fortius ("Swifter, Higher, Stronger"—The Olympics)
"To Seek Truth is Knowledge" (Madurai Kamaraj University, India)
"Unity in Diversity" (Republic of South Africa)
Veritas ("Truth"—Harvard University)
"Stretch for Excellence" (Columbine High School, Colorado)
Liberté, Égalité, Fraternité ("Liberty, Equality, Fraternity"—France)
"Our Mission and Values are to Help People and Businesses throughout the World Realize their Full Potential" (Microsoft)

"Dedicated to Truth" (University of Delhi, India)

Patet Omnibus Veritas ("Truth Lies Open to All"—Lancaster University, UK)

"Independence of Learning" (Waseda University, Tokyo, Japan)

Semper Fidelis ("Always Faithful"—United States Marine Corp)

These are just a few mottos and vision statements that come to mind. Some are better known than others are. Does your school have a vision statement or motto? How is it written, in the local language, English or Latin? If you have a motto, is it something you recite or repeat each day as part of a class or assembly ritual? Perhaps the most important question is: What does your school's motto mean to you personally? Have you ever discussed it with anyone? Reflecting a bygone era some of our greatest institutions have mottos that are written in Latin. These days too few of us speak Latin and, unless the motto is translated for us, we simply reproduce it on letter heads, flags, jerseys, or banners, nod our heads and continue with other more urgent business.

Mottos have lost their meaning. How do we resurrect them? If this means translating them into languages that everyone can easily recognize, or making the motto part of a school citizenship lesson that every pupil must pass, then that is what we must do. In some cases giving renewed meaning to an old motto is all a classroom needs to become transformational.

But we should not interpret flexibility as the opposite of stability. The two can work together. A flexible classroom is an adaptable classroom. However, stability must be built into every classroom. This is where core values come in. While we want our classrooms to be adaptive spaces, capable of responding to the changing needs of the individual, the marketplace, and the future; we also want these classrooms to be founded on cardinal principles that are not to be easily compromised by shifting agendas. In this regard classrooms are like other spaces or institutions in society. When they work well they combine the very best of traditions with a respect for change. Mottos or mission and vision statements capture traditions, honor and heritage while programs, policies, and personnel usually reflect change and adaptability.

INSTILLING AND INSPIRING TRUST

Trust allows students to become more effective values-based learners. Instilling trust as a cardinal virtue can be difficult. Some students will have a problem developing trust relationships because of emotional or physical issues in their pasts that have not been resolved. Before teachers can instill trust in their pupils something must be done to build a positive or receptive environment.

The chief barriers to the development of trust are failure to communicate and a negative attitude. Communication opens the door to an exchange of information between students and teachers or students and their classmates. Facilitating two-way communication frees students of the burden of guilt, from being misunderstood by others, and from their emotional pain.

Open communication is liberating and allows individual students to literally live again and believe in something greater than themselves. This is the first step to cultivating trust.

Communication though is not enough. Negativity is deeply rooted in society and expressed in many different ways. It is found in the gap is between what the adult world says is true or valued and what pupils actually see and experience. Basically, negativity can be interpreted as a credibility gap, or the unfairness and injustice that are perceived to exist in society. Resolving these deep-seated fears about society's stance on basic issues is not something accomplished in a single lesson, internship, or critical thinking seminar.

Getting students to regain their confidence in people, principles, and key institutions is an important goal of transformational learning. Confidence, integrity, values, and faith are connected. Building values into the heart of the classroom agenda helps mitigate problems of trust (Table 9.3).

Table 9.3: Overcoming Poor Communication and Negativity

Share	Be seen as a giver. Dispense freely of your knowledge, time, and compassionate interest.
Empathize	Meet students at their different points of need. Without abandoning your principles, try to see life from their point of view.
Emphasize the "Other" Perspective	Remember transformation is about developing others. In the process you too will be changed.
Promote two-way dialogue	Everyone has a story to tell. Listen out for these narratives and look for ways of giving voice to those who might otherwise remain silent.
Avoid making premature judgments	Do not rush to conclusions. Allow time for understanding.
Promote values	Work from your bedrock of principles and values. Identify these and be intentional about linking these values to classroom goals.
Promote justice as fairness	Define justice and fairness for yourself. Clarify the class's views on justice and fairness. Seek out opportunities to promote justice and fairness in the classroom (understanding, politeness, diversity, critical thinking, discipline, etc.)
Be consistent	Your integrity is at stake. Your students are watching you. Renew your commitment to core values and walk a steady path.
Practice what you preach	Align your words with your actions. Prove the application of your transformational agenda. As students say: Be ready to walk the talk.
Give good reasons for your philosophy of life	Be clear not only about your beliefs, but also about the "Why?" of your beliefs. Work on the principle that someone is going to ask questions. Be prepared to give answers.
Emphasize the importance of trust	Show how developing trust is necessary to build healthy relationships both inside and outside of the classroom.

Source: Authors.

If a single word can be used to represent trust that word is mutual. Because trust is a shared relationship, there must be a mutual understanding for it to succeed. Hidden motives and competing agendas all too often get in the way of building trust. These motives and agendas must be removed before trust can be established. The transformational journey is a journey of faith.

Transformational teachers inspire trust by showing their students that they care. Caring for students may not be the first priority on many teachers' agenda. This is even truer in an environment of reduced resources, time, professional emphasis and, in some communities, fear of parents or lawsuits. Teachers who are not afraid to show they care exhibit courage. Students who are valued as individuals are more likely to open up and contribute to developing a positive classroom culture. Caring begets trust, which in turn begets hope and confidence, leading to transformation (Figure 9.1).

Figure 9.1: The Journey from Caring to Transformation

Caring ⟶ Trust ⟶ Hope ⟶ Confidence ⟶ Transformation

Source: Authors.

Caring teachers are a rare commodity. Students remember them. Caring teachers who demonstrate the courage of their convictions are more likely to instill and inspire trust than others who play only to the chorus of their professional affiliations, or one-dimensional performance indicators.

In much the same way that the transformational classroom can be hijacked by grudge behavior, students who cannot be trusted limit the transformational capacities of the classroom (Table 9.4). This means that teachers are not the only ones required to show trust. Students too must be encouraged to embrace the benefits of being trustworthy. A trusting attitude goes hand-in-hand with the development of a trustworthy character.

Table 9.4: The Pull and Push of Transformation

PULL	PUSH
"Positive"	"Negative"
Developing	Challenging
Inspiring and instilling hope	Inspiring and instilling hope
Sharing, confiding	Autonomous, disciplined
Respect	Self-respect
Dependent	Accountable
Trusting	Trustworthy

Source: Authors.

Trusting and trustworthiness are two sides of the same transformational coin. Trusting is all about encouraging which elicits confidence. Trustworthiness is also about eliciting hope. But in this case individuals are pushed to a point where they embrace the critical and deeper value of being trustworthy. Change occurs in both situations. In one, the student has a need that the teacher seeks to meet through encouragement and a caring attitude. In the second, the student has a deeper values-need. This is where the transformation of character begins.

Teachers who build trust in their classroom promote trusting and trustworthy students with enhanced capacities to learn. When students and teachers exist in a parallel trust situation, building a transformational culture is discovered to be more than just a good idea. It becomes a physical possibility and concrete opportunity.

Silent Whispers

"I don't really care what Mr Gopal says about my attitude. He's a terrible teacher."

"Oh she's easy; you can get away with anything in her class."

"Mrs Rodriguez is a real stickler for turning in your homework on time."

"My favorite teacher is Mr Stone. I understand where he's coming from. And he understands me."

"I had this teacher in seventh grade that always pounded her fist on the desk to make a point. None of us dared approach her desk for help. We were too afraid."

"Mr Randall's a pushover. He let's us get away with anything."

"Our supply teacher's a weirdo!"

"If you're late for Mr Murtha's science class he makes you write a note of apology."

"Our Principal is always spouting off about what she thinks. She doesn't care about anything we have to say."

A HOLISTIC ENVIRONMENT

When we work on the whole individual the true benefits of transformational learning become evident. The dual "trusting-trustworthy" approach is revealed to be much more than a routine that leaders turn on and off depending on the circumstances. It is part of a carefully crafted strategy to instill change in the individual from the inside out.

Developing students' self-efficacy paves the way for these students to step up to their responsibility as active citizens of their communities. Beginning in the classroom they overcome their fears of failure and mistrust of institutions and authority. They regain confidence in their own and others' abilities to achieve. They see questions of fairness and justice as part of the daily lesson of life. More importantly, they appreciate the honest values-based answers that transformational teachers give. With increased self-efficacy comes an increased capacity to positively relate to others.

Trust building does more than wipe the slate of students' fears clean. It allows students to become infused with a set of new values that emanate from acceptance of the need for change. In trusting, they become trustworthy. The holistic environment extends beyond the individual and even the classroom. The character developed in the person and presented in the classroom over time becomes the same character found at home, at work, in society. Transformational learning helps build holistic transformational communities.

CONNECTING TRUST AND RESPECT

If you have some respect for people as they are, you can be more effective in helping them to become better than they are.

~ John W. Gardner

Trust and respect go together. Learning to trust helps to foster respect. In the classroom students who trust their teachers are more likely to show and command respect. Trust and respect are co-dependent.

SELF-RESPECT

Before transformational teachers and students can command or earn respect they must develop that special quality of self which is universally known as self-respect. The logic is simple: individuals who are broken up or less than "whole" on the inside find it difficult to give of their best. "Wholeness" and emotional well-being are important qualifiers of respect. Self-respect can be achieved in a variety of ways.

- Value: Questions of personal value and self-worth. This refers to an individual's inherent physical and emotional worth. Increasing this value increases self-respect. When this is lost or devalued we feel empty. A daily affirmation of values helps set our house of self respect in order. Faith or a personal belief system bolsters our estimation of value and can compensate for any temporary loss of value. When self says "I have no meaning" faith steps in to fill the gap.
- Integrity: The alignment of behavior with values. Similar to what was elsewhere referred to as "consistency," integrity is compromised every time the link between personal values and behavior is broken. Integrity exists when beliefs, ideals, principles or values are consistent or align with what others observe. In addition to what the world can see, integrity also covers ones thoughts and emotions. At the deepest level integrity embraces the compass points of life laid out in Chapter 1. The objective here is being at peace with self as well as others.
- Dignity: The quality of distinction. We tend to see dignity as simply another word for self-respect or self-worth. In some ways it is. However, there is an aspect of dignity that is worth separating from the more general perception. This is the quality of distinction or a healthy pride. In this case dignity is similar to the confidence we feel and exhibit. Not to be confused with showing off or bragging, dignity is essentially an attitude of mind that can be translated into action. Examples of dignity are found wherever individuals stand for something and display a quiet confidence of purpose. Every student, teacher, school, and community should be able to come up with a list of heroes, saints, gurus, and ordinary citizenry who illustrate well this quality of distinction.

- Excellence: Seeking quality in all things. Self-respect and mediocrity are natural enemies. Transformational teachers will work to communicate this fact to their students. Aiming to be the best in all things is a vow many make but very few keep. At least that is the impression we get from a review of history or analysis of contemporary life. The desire to excel must go beyond the expression of intentions. Commitment must be lived. Where is the proof? Show me your plan. Excellence is above all quality in action.

The trust and respect we expect to find in relationships between parents and children illustrates how trust and respect are linked. When children trust and have confidence in their parents, they are more likely to show their parents respect. The same is true for relationships between spouses, bosses and employees, military officers, politicians, and others. When relationships break down, the first casualty is the loss of respect and trust. The two are often linked in our minds. It is difficult to show respect for someone who has either breached our trust or whom we do not trust. Likewise, it is almost impossible to trust someone we do not respect. Make a list of your closet friends or colleagues. How many do you trust? How many do you respect? Be honest. How many of the names on your list would you omit from either the trust or respect column (Table 9.5)?

Table 9.5:   Linking Trust and Respect

Name	Trust	Respect
1.		
2.		
3.		
4.		
5.		

Source: Authors.

There should be a close correspondence between persons you respect and those you trust. If you're able to tick one item but not the other, more than likely, your level of trust or respect is not as high as you initially thought. Ask yourself why. The answer could be that you do not know the individual well enough. Or maybe you find it difficult to trust anyone, at least implicitly. Do you have trust issues? In this case, it might be useful to ask what criteria other than trust and respect you use to choose your friends.

Developing trust in the classroom helps instill respect. Respect is one of the outcomes of a trustworthy character. It is interesting that some of the more common words for respect are esteem, regard, and consideration. Each of these words can also be interpreted as value. Those we trust we tend also to value.

Trust + Respect = Value

Based on this calculation, trust and respect are necessary ingredients of transformational teaching. Typically, when we speak of respect, it is in relationship to students showing respect for their teachers. This is part of a common tendency to equate respect with deference. We associate respect with discipline, authority, and power; something that can be commanded. However, respect is a much more open concept. As we often say, respect is earned not given. Like trust, respect is a gift that can be extended to both parties in a relationship. To the extent that students and teachers are seen as partners, everyone benefits when trust and respect are maximized. And, over time, society is the net beneficiary.

THE GIFT OF TRUST

Nothing worthwhile in life has ever been achieved without a measure of sacrifice. The suggestions made above are only useful if teachers and students are willing to dialogue and commit. Developing trust is often a major battleground. Sometimes mistrust or distrust can be mistaken for the natural order of things. Suspicion and private agendas are what we have come to expect of others. Why should the classroom be any different? This cynical view of relationships and perhaps of society in general says something about the values we hold. Creating a general climate in which trust can flourish leads to more specific steps for resolving conflict.

In general, conflict is natural and to be expected. Looked at from one point of view, leadership of the classroom always takes place in the midst of conflict, which is a natural setting for transformational leadership. However, dealing with conflict head-on is not the same as achieving consensus. In a world driven by conflict, "thrashing out the issues" can be interpreted as thrashing the individual or trampling over another's' pride and self-respect. Achieving consensus should be the aim of transformational conflict resolution. As a teacher take into account the dynamics of conflict management, communication, negotiation and agreement (covenant). Stewart Levine encourages leaders to use a process that brings conflict into collaboration and resolution (Levine, 2009: 3–11).

This is what every classroom needs. The reasons are clear. Conflict is costly. In addition to thwarting trust and respect, conflict has a cost in lost emotional energy and reduced classroom productivity. And the costs beyond the classroom may be even greater. Like love, trust cannot be forced or compelled. It must be freely embraced. The benefits of conflict resolution should be made obvious. In the battle for the hearts and minds of students particularly regarding issues of discipline and attitude, trust can become a tug of war. All of this changes when it becomes clear that all sides have a more or less equal stake in resolving conflicts. Identifying this motivation is critical.

Conflict Resolution Techniques

- See conflict as natural: The tendency to view conflict as the enemy keeps everyone hiding behind a wall of unreality. It is unresolved conflicts that challenge peace in the classroom. Dealing with conflicts positively allows important issues to surface and be confronted in a climate of understanding. Conflicts can also point to important changes that may be taking place both inside and outside of school. Vulnerability is one of the traits transformational leaders openly embrace. Conflicts will very often expose this vulnerability and become a passageway into the soul of your classroom leading to the emergence of a deeper trust and respect.

- Think ahead: Leaders who know how to resolve conflicts and who think strategically have a head start over others who stumble into the classroom or make up the rules along the way.
- Establish a common ground: The class that works together stays together. Transformational leaders in the classroom resolve conflict and establish trust by building a community culture within the classroom. When teachers and students commit to working together the following outcomes can be expected:
  - Fewer personal conflicts and confusion.
  - Clear demarcation of roles and responsibilities.
  - More effective use of time.
  - Higher levels of performance through coordinated efforts.
- Face the issues: This is a good way of airing issues without putting any one individual on the spot (Table 9.6). Ask everyone in the class to write down on a separate piece of paper the main trust or other issue they would like to see resolved. Collect these papers then distribute them randomly. Each student gets to present the issue on the paper they have received. This works well in situations when individuals for a variety of reasons (fear, embarrassment, shyness,) may not want to bring up an issue. It keeps the issues anonymous, although students may opt to associate their names with a particular issue. However, the choice is theirs. Once the issues have been aired, develop an action plan that shows how the class as a whole will resolve the issues identified. Set a timeline that involves reporting back on progress made.

Table 9.6: Resolving Our Issues

The Issue	Agreed Action	Specific Benefit	Who? (appoint a leader)	Timetable
1.				
2.				
3.				

Source: Authors.

- Develop the art of storytelling: This is really the art of learning to role-play. By telling or acting a story students begin to think deeply about the issues under discussion. Every individual should be given the opportunity (but not forced) to role play. The idea here is to get students to play roles or handle situations other than the ones they are familiar with. In role playing each individual assumes the opinions and argues the issues of the character they are playing. This is one situation where good use can be made of any student's natural acting or even forceful personalities. Typically, this works best when individuals with strong opinions one way take on the role of someone with the opposite opinion. This leads to a debate of the issues and can help promote understanding and empathy.

- Learn to forgive: Release hurt anger and resentment. According to some authors, forgiveness is an important response to organizational conflict and restoration of relationships. Forgiveness is the alternative to revenge or holding onto anger which are dangerous responses. In the classroom forgiveness can be a good way to reconcile individuals who are experiencing the bitterness of interpersonal hurts and injustices.[1]

Conflict resolution techniques go hand-in-hand with classroom negotiation techniques. The two should be seen as part of an integrated trust building strategy (Figure 9.2).

Figure 9.2: Building Trust

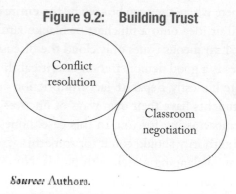

Source: Authors.

Classroom Negotiation Techniques

- Define your purpose: The purpose-driven classroom is built around a clear set of goals. Apart from the obvious curriculum goals that may be set, set a values and transformational purpose for the class. In other words, look beyond the curriculum to students' transformational needs. The more these needs are factored into your purpose the more prepared you will be to deal with the challenges that arise in the normal course of teaching. The technique in this case is no more complicated than thinking through your purpose in advance. Set a goal or set of goals and reduce those gray uncertain

---

[1] The following are interesting discussions on forgiveness: Bradfield, M. O., K. Aquino, and D. Stanwyck, "The Effects of Blame Attribution and Justice Violations on Revenge and Forgiveness in the workplace," Paper presented at the Academy of Human Resource Development Conference, Atlanta, Georgia (1997, March); Butler, D. S., "The Effects on Personality and General Health on Choosing Interpersonal Forgiveness in the Workplace, Doctoral dissertation (Dissertation Abstracts International, Georgia: Georgia State University, 1997), 58, 4498; McCullough, M. E., and E. L. Worthington Jr., "Encouraging Clients to Forgive People who have Hurt Them: Review, Critique, and Research Prospectus," *Journal of Psychology and Theology* 22, (1994): 3–20.

moments. Students will come to value the importance of direction and be more willing to trust.

- The issues: Avoid getting caught up in petty classroom wrangling. If negotiation is required then identify the issues up front. Define them as clearly as possible and make sure they represent the different parties involved. Even if others want to drag everything else into the ring, say no. Identify the important issues. Focus on these and forget the others. The critical issues are those which, if not addressed, may escalate. Clustering is a useful technique to use in deciding on the main issues. Hand out two or three cards to everyone. Ask students to write down what they think are the main issues using one card for each issue. Limit the number of words that can be used. This isn't the time for mini essays. Collect the completed cards. Shuffle them. Read out each card then arrange them somewhere where they can be seen by the entire class (it may be a good idea to transfer each card or idea onto a flipchart or blackboard). When negotiating, stick to the agreed issues. Extraneous issues only cloud the discussion and confuse everyone. Sticking to the issues is a good demonstration of critical thinking skills.

- Be honest: Negotiate honestly. Separate fact from fiction and tell the truth. If you do not know, say so. Students have their own ways of uncovering the truth which can be more than a little embarrassing for you. In this case, honesty really is the best policy. While the teacher's authority should count for something, resist the temptation to rest on this. Don't get into a slanging match with pupils. No matter how you look at this, you will always lose. Even if your students don't say it, they hold you to a higher standard. Dishonesty is the quickest way to lose your bargaining power with students. It also erodes your self-respect.

- Team: Resist the common tendency to split the class up into camps. Schools are already fertile grounds for a variety of in and out-groups, cliques, gangs, clubs, and other divisions based on age, skin color, gender, ethnic background, religion, music preference, dress, academic performance, etc. Don't add to these by creating additional divisions or endorsing divisions that students sometimes bring to school. Divisions get in the way of an ability to negotiate and establish trust. Find other ways to integrate the class. Create a class motto, establish a sharing routine where individuals are free to speak about something important to them, rotate special duties, and develop a class brand loyalty.

- Think win-win: Approach negotiation with a sense of inclusiveness. How can everyone benefit? Rather than classifying people as winners and losers think of different kinds or levels of benefits. Negotiation does not have to be seen as a zero-sum game where one side's gains are automatically chalked up as losses for the other.

- Negotiation implies trade-offs. In negotiating trust or respect can you list different categories or units of value? How can these be distributed so that everyone becomes a winner? Take an obvious case of discipline. A student is repeatedly tardy. Depending on your particular school's rules, you can either penalize the student (which might be seen as a win-lose result) or, assuming there are no compelling reasons for the student's lateness, develop a pact with the student that encourages them to take individual responsibility. By negotiating the terms of the lateness "agreement" and the outcomes students are made aware of their control over the situation. Win or "lose" students gain the understanding of self-respect and trustworthiness. The same principle can be applied to other more serious infractions of school rules or classroom conduct.

- Synergize: Synergy is usually summed up in the expression that the whole is greater than the sum of its individual parts. This is akin to saying that the wheel of a bicycle is more useful than the individual spokes. In part, this is what the focus on teamwork is all about. Encouraging everyone to pull together in the same direction, should reduce the natural tensions that arise from competing agendas. Instead of the negotiation being between you and your students or between different groups of students, present it rather as a class negotiation. The negotiation takes places within the class camp. The advantage of this approach is it builds on the individual strengths or abilities of all without necessarily emphasizing one over the other. It is the general class result we are interested in. One plus one is shown to equal three. The usual fear in developing synergy within the class is that teachers will play to the lowest common denominator usually because not everyone will pull their weight equally. This negative assessment ignores the fact that everyone brings different skills to the negotiating table. One student's critical thinking skills are another's compassion. Or where one student is more disposed to share, another may be more forgiving. Computing these different qualities can be a full-time task. However, what is important is the pooled result. Infusing trust into the process is a continuous task. By focusing on synergy transformation is made a collective undertaking. The message is that in working together we derive greater benefits than could ever be achieved if we worked alone.

DEVELOPING A ROUTINE

Everyone brings a unique personality to the classroom. Backgrounds, experiences, expectations, and levels of commitment are different. Sorting through these differences takes time. Trust and respect should be viewed as major transformational objectives. As an "encourager," you will teach students to trust and confide their ambitions. This raises the level of hope in your class. Encouraging teachers bring out the best in their students using positive reinforcement techniques and modeling the right behavior. However, encouragement is only one part of the role transformational teacher's play when developing trust. It is also important to point out the connection between trust and respect.

Respect comes from trusting. It builds on developing students' characters. Individuals learn not only to trust but to be trustworthy and worthy of respect. Transformation is the work of a lifetime. Trust is the same. The quality of student–teacher and student–student relationships and emotional happiness improves the more trusting and trustworthy everyone is. All the virtues commonly sought in relationships with others—honesty, confidence, commitment, loyalty, and respect—are found to be built on trust.

CONCLUSION—BUILDING A CLASSROOM WITH TRUST

In many places today trust is a foreign word. We are pleasantly surprised when our leaders, family members, friends and others invoke the message of trust. Even more surprising is when they live up to the promise of their words. Trust seems to be the exception to a more general rule of mistrust, distrust, cynicism and, perhaps worst of all, fear. Our classrooms reflect the reality of our communities. The global implications of any attempt to increase trust should be obvious. By building trust into the classroom we sow seeds of hope in the citizens of tomorrow. Today's student can be tomorrow's ambassador for good. In a world that too often appears to be punctuated by invective, name calling, and naked aggression, the potential for trust to redefine the terms upon which relationships are built is staggering. This is part of what was meant in our Preface where we suggested that the classroom could be the most powerful space on earth. Given the importance of trust, what are some specific steps we can take to build a classroom with trust?

Building trust and earning respect is a daily battle. Any of the following can be implemented without fanfare and with no more resources than most classrooms and schools will already have at their disposal. The really important tool necessary to bring each of these suggestions to life is commitment.

Declare your **Commitment**
How deep is your commitment to building a trust-filled environment?

Learn the fine art of **Communication**
How well do you communicate? Are you an active listener?

Collaborate with **Others**
How deep is your commitment?

Model trust
Are you modeling the trust you expect of others?

Clear steps on the road to building or establishing trust include:

✓ **Step 1:** Good manners—Rude behavior has never won friends. Even though the rules of proper behavior (deportment) and etiquette are external behaviors and continue to change, being polite is still a good way to gain trust and command respect. Make a commitment to being polite. List 3 ways you will daily show respect to others.
✓ **Step 2:** Show consideration for others—Success is found in building positive relationships. Consideration of others means less selfish thinking. Spread your wings. Extend your friendship circle. Increase your awareness of others. Work from the premise that everyone has value. Think of at least one thing you value in your students (students should do the same for teachers). Now work on extending this list.

✓ **Step 3:** Watch your language—Apart from the actual words we use (avoid cursing and blaming), watching the tone of one's voice is important. A harsh tone will usually fuel resentment, which works against cultivation of respect and trust. Work on eliminating hateful, discriminatory, crude, and other inappropriate words from your vocabulary. Smile more often and be more welcoming in your language and tone.

✓ **Step 4:** Avoid gossip—This appears on almost everyone's no-no list. Yet gossip continues to gain favor wherever two or more people are gathered whether in face-to-face or electronic conversation. Gossiping is really part of the "mind your language" step above. However, it is important enough to be listed separately. Avoid rumor mills. Do not spread tales, or stories about others you know to be untrue. A good rule of thumb is, "If in doubt, cut it out." Encourage others to do the same. Contrary to the popular saying, sticks and stones can be very hurtful and earn few if any trust or respect bonus points.

✓ **Step 5:** Serving—Classrooms are team environments. It makes sense to find ways of collaborating with others in a joint task. Rephrasing President John Kennedy's famous quote: "Ask not what others can do for you, rather ask what you can do for others." What can you do to help others? Think practically. Sharing, coaching, mentoring, or simply being patient with others, offers unlimited opportunities for nurturing respect and cultivating trust.

✓ **Step 6:** Set high standards—For yourself as well as for others. Making a commitment to excellence is an obvious way to earn the respect of others. Setting high standards is another way of letting others know the importance attached to quality and other principles. Additionally, a commitment to being the best one can be is yet another way of signaling self respect. Living up to one's fullest potential covers both external and internal qualities and reflects on everything from deportment and punctuality to grades, team spirit, participation in extra-curricular activities, attitude, and character.

Taken together, these steps force a review of the central question: Who am I? Am I trusting, cynical, caring, critical, complacent, intolerant, collaborative, apathetic, arrogant, domineering, or dangerous? How do others perceive me? Why do I care? What trust footprints do we leave in our classrooms and communities? Do we have any followers? In addition to this, the other important question is: What do we really wish to accomplish?

Say it out "loud" so others can hear. Better yet, practice what you preach.

How much trust do we have in our own trust wishes? This is the question we cannot escape. What is the value of our accumulated investment in trust? How deep is your trust?

10

Emotional Fortitude

Hope sees the invisible, feels the intangible, and achieves the impossible.
~Anonymous

STRATEGY: GENERATE EMOTIONAL CREDIBILITY

BUILDING EMOTIONAL FORTITUDE

Emotions are complex. They drive most of our actions and have powerful consequences. They are associated with our thoughts, feelings and behavior and for many can wreak havoc on stability. As leaders, you have a responsibility to understand your own emotional endurance so that you can develop it as a potent value. By recognizing emotional fortitude as a value you can intentionally build your own strengths. If you develop your resources in this vital area, you will be able draw on your stability to help others gain theirs.

Emotional fortitude can be a strategic vehicle in forming a strong foundation for transformational leadership. What is our definition for emotional fortitude? Emotional fortitude is the ability to harness thoughts, feelings and behavior and leveraging them through insightful strength. The two operative words here are, harness and leverage.

To harness something is to bring it under control. Thoughts and feelings in themselves have a lot of energy (Sanders, 1998: 128). We are our thoughts and feelings. Thoughts and feelings must be directed in a way that will make them work for us. The intentional process of routing our thoughts and feelings in a certain direction allows us to accomplish tasks. The direction that thoughts and feeling are routed also results in behavior. If thoughts and feelings are not harnessed they can run freely. The free reign of thoughts and feelings causes irrational and immature behavior. If you examine you own emotions you will see that certain triggers cause you to react a certain way. If you don't learn how to control the triggers that lead to a particular reaction you become crippled by your own thoughts.

Leverage is strategic advantage. If you leverage something you intentionally move it in a direction; you affect or alter the circumstance. Leveraging our emotions is a way to not only gain control, but alter them so that they can accomplish a task or behavior (Muchinsky, 2003: 434). When a person uses a mechanical device called a lever, he can stand at a distance to maneuver an object in the direction he desires it to go. The same is the case with our emotions. In a sense, we can use an intentional process to maneuver our feelings and thoughts allow ourselves to change and move in a different direction.

The building blocks for emotional fortitude are simple. We will break it down into three basic parts. We will look at the parts of emotional fortitude as steps to take to build and grow. This exercise will help you to take a look at how you can harness and leverage your thoughts and emotions toward more desirable outcomes.

In your SWOT notebook under your Goal section set up a new page called Emotional Fortitude. In one column on the left-hand-side of the page write the word Courage. At the top of the middle of the page write Endurance, and at the top of the right hand write Determinaion.

STEP ONE: COURAGE

Courage is the ability to face difficult situations. Most people have courage to some degree. It may be difficult for you to recognize the areas that you have courage until you recognize areas where you are weak. Here are some signs that you may have a weak area in courage:

- You procrastinate.
- You have fear.
- You have trouble making decisions.
- You fear that your decisions are not valid.
- You worry.
- You fret.
- You feel ill when faced with certain situations.
- You continually run the thoughts of unpleasant circumstances through your mind.
- You avoid people.

Under the heading of Courage write down any of the areas that apply to you and put a letter "W" after them signifying that you are weak in this area. You may add other areas to your list that apply to you personally.

If on the other hand you are a person that has the ability to face difficult situations then you will want to identify your areas of strength. As you identify and list your areas of strength put an "S" after them. Here are some examples. Again, add your own areas to your list. This will help you to see the areas of strength and the areas of weakness that you will work on in the future.

- You are bold.
- You are fearless.
- You have tenacity.
- You have spunk.

- You have the heart of a lion.
- You are daring.
- You are hearty.

STEP TWO: ENDURANCE

The second step in building emotional fortitude is endurance. Endurance is the power to withstand hardship and stress. Again, you are going to put a "W" after areas of weakness and an "S" after areas of strength.

- If you have difficulty with endurance you may exhibit the following weakness.
- You cry easily.
- You get nervous often.
- You seek other's approval continually.
- You seek vices to help you cope.
- You feel that you need others to help you frequently.
- You have difficulty completing simple tasks.
- You feel depressed.
- You feel angry frequently.
- You hold grudges.

Again, being honest with your list will help you to identify the areas that you will need to boost to get personal leverage.

The following list is examples of strength in the area of endurance. Add these or others that you can identify to your personal list.

- You see challenges as exciting opportunities.
- You recognize areas of stress and seek creative ways to handle it.
- You analyze hardship and look for the silver lining.
- You wake up excited about the possibilities each day brings.
- You look at the past with positive thoughts.
- You look forward to the future.
- You forgive others as they hurt you.
- You do not fret over what others are doing.
- You do not worry about the future.
- You don't obsess about things you can't control.

STEP THREE: DETERMINATION

The third step in leveraging your emotional fortitude is determination. Determination is the act of making up your mind about something (Canfield, 2005: 130–38). Some people see determination as a stubborn tenacity to hang or a strong will. The determination that build emotional fortitude is a little of stubborn tenacity but it is also the ability to have healthy conviction. Here is an example of healthy determination that you might add to your strengths.

- You have a strong belief system.
- You proceed in key areas of your life with certainty.
- You have strong faith.
- You are not afraid to act on your beliefs.
- You are willing to stand firm in the face of difficulty.
- You don't give up easily.
- You make sound judgments when asked to make decisions.
- You are persistent when you encounter obstacles.

Here are some examples of weak determination:

- You are uncertain about your beliefs.
- You follow a crowd easily even if you think they are wrong.
- You worry about your ability to control your future.
- You second guess your decisions.
- If you encounter opposition to your ideas you quickly give up on them.
- You allow others to criticize you and you internalize their comments.
- You lack direction in your life.

After you've completed these lists transfer them into your strength and weakness sections of your SWOT notebook. You have now discovered areas that you are emotionally strong and areas that you are emotionally weak. If you analyze each area that you listed you will begin to see a pattern in your emotional stability. The good news about emotions is that they can be harnessed and they can be leveraged so that you can develop. Let's take a look at the three steps of developing emotional fortitude. Honestly engaging in understanding these three vital areas will help you to develop emotional fortitude as a value and a strategy to help others.

Courage

Eli was only nine years old when he was diagnosed with Leukemia. His parents were devastated. When the doctor called Eli's parents in to break the bad news they had a range of emotions. They were fearful and sad. They felt angry and hurt that this could happen to their beautiful child. They wondered how they would tell Eli that he would have to go through treatments. As they explored their options they realized that they would have a big part in helping Eli to get well. One of the keys to his treatment would be his attitude. The doctor explained that attitude plays a big part of successful recovery. The treatments would be more effective if Eli went into them with a feeling that he could beat the disease. Mental readiness was imperative.

Eli's parents struggled. They never faced anything like this before. They were not prepared to receive such harsh news about their loved son. Eli's mother, Marta was a woman with strong faith. She believed that her son could be healed. Eli's father Joseph never embraced faith and was doubtful. He became sick with worry and withdrew. He could not see how he would have the courage to face his son's disease. He spent several nights fretting about the possible outcomes of Eli's situation. He could not think about the possibilities of a positive outcome because he was overcome with grief and sorrow.

Something changed Joseph. In the midst of his lack of courage he remembered what the doctor said. "Eli will have a much better chance at successful treatment if he has a good attitude." Joseph realized that his own lack of courage would be a detriment to Eli's recovery.

Courage is facing the unknown with hope.
It is facing the unknown with strength of purpose.

The difference between people who have courage and the people that don't is hope and strength of purpose. For Joseph, it was hard to have hope because he didn't have faith. However, he knew that courage is born from having love. He loved Eli. He wanted to do the right thing. He faced the darkness of the unknown and stepped forward with the conviction that we would help Eli face the unknown by standing by his side.

Courage is the ability to face uncertainty with conviction. Courage is deciding that you will have emotional strength (Daft, 2002: 219). No one can make you have courage. No one can decide for you that you will take on your challenges with boldness. If you are willing to stand up to the unknown and accept that outcomes may be beyond your control then you have courage.

When Joseph and Marta determined ahead of time that they would face Eli's future with courage they became strong. They showed the people around them that they were in control of their feelings and emotions and their behavior followed. Instead of fretting each day and feeling miserable, Joseph and Marta planned ways to make the most of their son's days. They planned little trips and celebrated every day as a victory. Others were drawn toward them as they demonstrated their ability to face the days with joyful thoughts.

Eli grew from the experience. When he saw his parent's courage he rested in their strength. Joseph and Marta taught Eli how to face the unknown. Their son felt their joy and didn't dread his treatments. Instead of losing the precious time they had left with Eli with grief and sadness, they lived life to its fullest. Joseph and Marta were astonished at their own ability to cope with the stresses they continued to face. In the beginning, their choice toward a bold approach to looking on the bright side was difficult. They had to struggle at their attempts to smile. Before long they started noticing little things around them that brought joy. Soon they became less self absorbed and began to see the need of others. They became a source of inspiration by simply taking a blind step toward the unknown with hope and a true sense of purpose.

If you think about your own circumstances you will realize a truth that will help you to face your unknowns. All circumstances must be faced with courage. All circumstances in life have the same element of the unknown. Since we can never be totally sure abut any outcome we have to face everything with and element of hope and the strength of purpose. Strength of purpose is that we have a Creator that cares about everything that we do and we can trust that our lives have a unique purpose. We may not understand our purpose but we can rejoice and be glad that our journey of courage is part of the purpose.

As Joseph and Marta harnessed their emotions, they were able to stand back and assess how they would benefit Eli. They used leverage to move their circumstances toward a positive outcome. Eli benefited by learning the value of emotional strength from his parents. He felt loved and hopeful until the day that they had to say goodbye.

Endurance

Do you know anyone who has not faced stress? Can you think of a single sole that has not been confronted with hardship? Stress and hardship are part of life. Part of endurance is learning how to face hardship and stress and pacing yourself so that you can go the distance. The key to endurance is twofold. The first is that you have to condition yourself for the long run and the second it to have the patience to hang in there as you are making your way through the long run. No matter what you face, your ability to exhibit great emotional endurance will boost your confidence and aid others.

Emotional conditioning is just like the conditioning needed for an athlete. Emotional health requires a balanced life style with plenty of exercise, good nutrition, and rest. One of the key ingredients to emotional conditioning is realizing that if the balance bar is tipped everything will slide to one end. You know the story. If you are feeling stressed and one thing goes wrong, almost everything else seems to follow in that direction. The reason that many things will fall apart at one time is that we fill our lives with too many responsibilities. Keeping a balanced lifestyle requires effort (Covey, 2004: 287). Just like the athlete who trains for endurance, our life has to have discipline and a sense of purpose. If you examine the answers you gave on your endurance column you will have a clue to what area of your life is out of balance.

Kara is a typical working mother. She teaches school and has three young daughters. She takes one daughter to day care every morning and then heads to school with her other two. She feels fortunate to have her daughters in the same school that she works. "My days are so hectic," Kara said when we asked her to describe her lifestyle. "I get up every morning at 5:00 a.m. to help my husband with the lunches. He helps me get the girls dressed and we try to have breakfast together before we head off for the day. Three days a week we have lessons. My older daughter has ballet on Wednesdays and my younger daughter has piano on Saturdays. I take the four year old to language lessons on Tuesdays. My husband and I go to the gym on alternate days so that we can spend some time with the girls. I have a book club that I like to attend once a month and my husband plays golf at least once a month. Since I teach, I have prep work on the weekend and papers to grade. We all pitch in and clean the house and work on the yard every week. But we try to do that as a family."

"Are you tired?" I asked. "That seems like a busy schedule."

Kara sighed, "Yes." She paused. "It's not that we are tired. I feel angry so much of the time. I don't get enough sleep and I never feel like I catch up. If we do cut something out we feel that we aren't keeping up with everyone. I know that I am depressed and I yell too much at the kids. Every day seems like we are on a tread mill and I don't see an end. I talk about it with my friends. We are all doing the same thing. I mean, where is the quality of life?"

Kara feels as if she is running and endurance race but is she enduring? Not according to our definition of endurance. Kara isn't building emotional reserve to withstand hardship and stress. She is stressed to the point of causing her own hardship. This is the case with most modern households. Many of the stress that people feel in their life is self induced. If Kara were to add a serious illness, loss of job or other life altering circumstance, she would be at the brink of an emotional collapse. The reason—Kara hasn't learned to pace herself for endurance.

The key to enjoying emotional health is to understand what it takes to complete the long race. The balanced lifestyle takes into account that down time is required. Time to reflect and understand and ponder the little things in life seems like a waste of time to many. Endurance requires careful planning. If you want to have emotional strength, look at your list for endurance and examine the areas of weakness. Plan to eliminate the areas of your life that are keeping you from a balanced lifestyle. If you don't take control, the stress factor will. It will cause you to lose control. Breaking apart emotionally causes long-term damage.

Leaders take control of their lives by first transforming their own life so that they can be an example to others. If you are trying to help other with emotional endurance, you need to be able to clearly demonstrate how it is done (Goleman, 2002: 46–47). If you are full of angst and worry, you will have nothing to say to others who suffer with the same pain. You will only commiserate.

Changing your life toward balance is a process. Think of it like a freight train. The train may be long and carrying several caboose cars with it. Each car has as emotional baggage. The stresses that come with the baggage add unhappiness and pain. The train is headed in one direction and the locomotive driving it is heavy and it pulls the cars along dutifully. There is a great amount of energy needed to power the locomotive. The first thing that has to be done is to examine each car and realize its contents. You might have to unhook the car and release it. The lighter the train the easier it will move and the less power it will need to get it where it is going.

The process of unhooking the cars with the baggage requires a hard look at the each area of life that consumes your time. Just as you budget your money; think of your time as a valuable resource as well. Your time can be linked to your values in that if you do not budget it wisely, just like money, you will not have enough to take care of the important things in your life.

Leaders learn how to budget their time wisely and set aside time for interruptions. Making yourself available for others requires that your time is not filled to the brink of overflow. Everyone heard that life is short and we should make the most of it. Making the most of courage is to have the strength to order your days. When you are able to demonstrate balance others will see that you value your time and theirs as well.

Determination

Determination is a great tool for emotional fortitude. It builds character. The key ingredient in determination is setting goals toward a clearly defined target. Setting clear goals and outlining the steps to reach the goals aids in stabilizing your focus. Determination recognizes that the path to reach the target may change. Flexibility is essential. It is very difficult to plan for every eventuality in life. As much as we would like to be in control of all of our details, the truth is, we cannot. For some people this fact is a source of continual frustration and worry and fear set in. Once worry and fear get a stronghold it is hard to break their hold. Having a true sense of your convictions will help you to face inevitable adversity.

People who are determined have a clear sense of success. The key to success is to define what the idea of success means to you. If you can have a clear sense of your own purpose in determining success you will have the underpinnings of direction. Once you know exactly what you want and the route that you intend to take it is up to you and you alone to step toward your vision.

Examine the statements made by the following people. These people, like many have a story of adversity and obstacles to overcome. As you read about them, jot down a few of the key ingredients that allowed them to achieve their vision of success.

Kjell—Norway: I lived in a remote fishing village located 250 miles north of the Arctic Circle. Our family had limited resources and I was determined to become a great musician. I found a woman in my village that played violin for the Oslo Orchestra. I bartered with her for lessons. She needed her roof fixed and I needed to learn to play. It wasn't my goal to play violin but she was the only person in our village with an instrument. After ten years of study she arranged for me to be a guest violist for an orchestra in Oslo. To me, it seemed that having only one teacher was an impediment to my success. But the orchestra said I had a unique and fresh style. I have been with the orchestra for five years now and have a dozen students. If I had not been believed in my vision my father and brothers would have talked me into being a fisherman. I know I would have been frustrated all of my life. It took hard work but I live the life that I dreamed of as a boy.[1]

Kristine—Latvia: I was orphaned when I was five. I lived in a very run down orphanage. We had little to eat and our education was limited. I began to dream about living in another country and having a wonderful education. I did not know how that dream could be realized. One day we were told that we would be able to participate in a program where we could visit with a host family in another country with the possibility of adoption. A counselor interviewed me and asked me to make a list of my special qualities. At first I couldn't think of anything that was special about me but then I realized that I love to help people. From that day on, I started to help everyone that I could. I started dreaming about being a nurse and read everything that I could in our small library about medicine. It wasn't long until I was making lists of things that I should do to help others. The orphanage found me a host family and I shared my lists with them. They loved me and adopted me. Today we work on my lists together. I know that one day, I'll be a nurse. The day that changed my life was the day I began to believe in my dream.[2]

---

[1] Fictional scenario based on a real-life case study to iterate the author's point.
[2] See footnote 1.

Su Lin—China: I came to the U.S. with my mother in 2001. My mother had relatives who gave her a job. At first, I felt very inferior to other people because of my accent and poor English. I enrolled in an ESL program and met many nice people who helped me to overcome my speech difficulties. One of my instructors taught me a valuable lesson. To this day I am practicing what she taught. I want to share her advice with you.

- Believe in yourself.
- Set goals—believe in them.
- Don't be afraid to dream—visualize the dream daily.
- Take a step toward your vision every day and write down your progress.[3]

The three people in these stories had the same thing in common. Each of them was not afraid dream. They took the necessary steps to visualize their dream so that when an opportunity presented itself, they were ready to move forward. They worked hard toward their goals and realized that the journey required them to be adaptable. Adapting to circumstances, while remaining in control of emotions, opens doors of opportunity.

Imagine if Kjell waited for the perfect opportunity to become a musician. He may have wallowed in self pity for a lifetime believing that he lived too far away from other musicians or that they were too poor. Kjell would have missed his opportunity because he closed himself emotionally by second guessing his dream.

Kristine may never have realized her dream if she didn't take stock of her own special qualities and capitalize on her specific strengths. Her opportunity was in her own hands to make lemonade out of the lemons in her life. She put one foot in front of the other with few resources. By maintaining a positive attitude she reached out to others and in turn helped herself toward her goal.

Su Lin recognized that her attitude affected her success as well. Her circumstances changed when she assessed her weakness and began working toward a goal of excellence that pleased her. She was willing to let others help her and didn't allow circumstances hold her down. Su Lin adapted to her new environment and changed her future.

Leaders take charge through determination. Transformational leaders help others to see the need to define clear goals, take risks, move forward, and be adaptable. Values are born from determination. Su Lin, Kjell, and Kristine all learned the value of hard work. They also learned to take risk by being involved in change. Change is an inevitable outcome of living. Transformational leaders help people to see that change has a purpose if you are will to shape the change by being actively engaged in the process.

TOOLS TO IGNITE GROWTH

Emotional credibility is the act of demonstrating authentic and reliable emotional stability. Leaders who demonstrate authentic and reliable emotional skill set the stage for growth

---

[3] Fictional scenario based on a real-life case study to iterate the author's point.

in followers. One of the key tools in helping followers to adapt to change is to create an atmosphere for emotional healing.

Most people have some type of emotional trauma in their life. Some people are able to deal with their trauma by ignoring it. Others are creative in turning their lemons into lemonade. Still others can carry around their pain and find themselves fixed in time, unable to change and adapt. Emotional trauma stunts growth in all organizations. Leaders should recognize that emotions play a major factor in every day life. Some people are more emotionally stable than others. This fact should be one that every leader acknowledges so that a viable strategy can be put in place. It is important to develop a viable strategy so that you can grow your organization or classroom to be emotionally healthy rather than emotionally ill.

Some leaders cause emotional trauma in their followers. Leaders who cause trauma rarely succeed as good leaders. They don't have the maturity to lead others to a higher level of growth. Enabling others to move forward is a noble value. It promotes healthy relationships and allows individuals to meet their goals. Setting an emotional growth strategy will motivate your followers and protect your organization from failure. A transformational leader can fill their followers with hope by igniting growth. People that are motivated are on the move. They create change. They crave change. They use change as an opportunity to perform.

Let's look at a few tools that will help you use emotional credibility as a strategy. There are three main tools to build this strategy. By using these tools you will help individuals to define their own need for growth as well as help others in their growth process. It should be noted that you, as a leader cannot solve everyone's emotional problems. What you need to be concerned with is giving your followers the tools to solve their own problems by recognizing the solution and moving forward.

Skill Set 1: Set Emotional Standards

What goes around comes around.

Did you ever hear the idiom "What goes around comes around?" This phrase means if you do something wrong to another person, it will come back and harm you as well. This idiom has a lot of truth.

There are two skill sets that we would like you to gain from this idiom.

1. Insight into the present: The present is filled with opportunity for growth. If you can help people to see the big picture you will help them to become more emotionally mature. What is the big picture? The big picture is that each day has value unto itself. The way that you treat people today, the value that you place on the presence in your life today, has in impact on your future as well as theirs. By building hope in those around you and helping them to see their worth you will also build your hope. It is easy to criticize and find fault with others. It is the way of mankind. But as you find fault, others will find fault with you. How you judge others, you will be judged. If you open

your heart to recognizing the worth of others you will help them to be healed from their emotional traumas. If you add to their harm you set your heart against your own emotional healing because they will not trust you or place their hope in your ability to lead them forward.

2. Foresight into the future: How you envision the people around you today will affect their ability to be motivated toward and ennobling future. That is, if you stunt their growth by belittling their present state you are binding them for a better future state. Successful visions need people to carry them out. The dynamics of change are altered if your communication results in crises. To draw a vision of success builds the people around you to be successful (Sanders, 1998: 90–92).

Skill Set 2: Nourish your Followers

The center of an egg is the yolk.

The egg yolk or the center of the egg is the food source. The leader is like a yolk. The yolk has to be the source of nourishment. You can nourish your followers by consistency. Consistency means that the framework that you set up should show stability. You can build stability by recognizing other's contributions as you move toward common goals. When followers don't understand the way a leader is taking them they become confused. The natural path of confusion is for a sub-leader, one that is not designated as the leader to take control. If you nourish your followers with consistency, clearly set goals and a recognition of their contributions, you will find your leadership to be successful. Don't hold back of feeding your followers. They must be fed by someone. They will go where they get the best nourishment. In other words, know the needs of your followers and provide their need of good leadership.

Skill Set 3: Stand Strong

Trees with deep roots stand through storms.

Trees with deep roots are able to stand when the winds, rain and cold threaten their structure. Leaders who have good emotional stability have good roots. In order to stand strong you should understand that stable emotions help others to feel safe. There is a relationship between order and stability and disorder and instability. In order for people to adapt in ever changing environments some things must be stable. Creating deep-rooted stability is a day by day process. Understand that small events lead to the bigger picture. If each circumstance causes a crises reaction, the whole of the parts will be reactive and unstable. Visa versa, if each circumstance is greeted with an attitude of excitement and creativity, you will teach your followers to dig deeper for solutions.

Filling the gap between the stable environment and unstable environment is relatively easy. It does not have to be complex. The main point is to foster creativity. Instead of viewing challenges as problems, view them as opportunities for maturity. Outline them for your followers and teach them how to view challenges with open hearts. Closed hearts are confused and frightened. Open hearts look for solutions.

PARTICIPATIVE LEADERSHIP

Transformational leaders recognize their role in building strong collaborations. Building strong collaborations is an intentional process. There are several ways to formulate a strong strategy of alliances that build emotional credibility.

1. Select honest people: In order to build strong emotional alliances you must pick people who are honest and demonstrate integrity. By surrounding yourself with honest people your leadership will manifest natural credibility. When you have selected people for their integrity you should let them know that it is your intention that everyone is accountable to one another. For some people, the idea of having a group of people that are accountable is a daunting task. Emotional credibility as a strategy relies on the presumption that the people that lead can trust you. Living a morale life in front of your followers builds credibility. Long-term credibility strengthens others to live morale lives as well. It teaches that there is hope. It helps followers to believe in themselves as leaders as well. Honesty enables people to explore their strengths and celebrates growth.

2. Build character: You can build your followers by helping them to build their character. Outline clear standards and help your followers set goals to meet those standards. One of the best ways to build good character in your followers is to teach them the basic pillars of character. Teach them to respect each other and honor one another's unique differences. Demonstrate caring by being kind and generous with one another. Offer forgiveness when needed and show your appreciation for other's contributions. Explain the purpose of sharing responsibility when needed and taking responsibility for your own actions. Iterate the power of cooperation and honoring the authority that governs your organization. Building character will build emotional stability as people see that what they do affects others deeply (Goleman, 2002: 14).

3. Build trust: Building trust is not easy. People want to believe that they can trust their leaders. Your followers will watch all of your actions to decide if they can trust you. If they don't believe that they can it is almost impossible to win them back. That is why the steps of building character and honesty must be at the top of the list. Followers may not say that they don't trust you but their actions will speak loudly. If you have a hard time winning them to your ideas, you will know that trust isn't present. Trust is the absence of suspicion. That being said, in order to build trust you must be above board in all of your actions. If you say one thing and do another, your credibility goes down. One of the ways that you can show your followers that they can trust you is by

communicating your actions. Clearly set up the standards that you expect that you and they will follow. Review the standards frequently weaving them into your vision, mission, and goals. Write them out for all to see and follow them meticulously.

4. Support positive interaction: Authentic positive interaction is a life-giving force. Everyone wants to feel that they are appreciated and that their ideas have worth. The leader sets the stage for positive interaction amongst peers. Leaders who show an interest in their followers equally send a message for others to follow. If a leader demonstrates a spirit of favoritism they risk creating an atmosphere of emotional instability. Followers who feel devalued are less productive and worry more about inconsequential circumstances. Not every leader can spend time with all of the people that are in their sphere of influence. The hierarchy that the leader sets up should be carefully monitored to ensure that there is a climate of trust and honesty. Gossip and unhealthy coalitions should be monitored as they are the breeding ground of discontent.

5. Adjust with change: One of the most important gifts a leader can give followers is the ability to adjust to change. Most people do not like change and we go to great lengths to try to avoid change. The fact is nothing stays the same from day to day. Building a climate of affirmation helps people to accept the unknown. If you build a culture that supports change then your followers will be more adaptable. If you set up a culture that celebrates victories and delights in change, you will find that you have followers that are ready to be motivated. They will also be ready for new ideas and visions. Rewarding followers for creative thinking will build emotional health and aid them in building their courage, endurance, and determination.

6. Create balance: Emotional balance is a necessity. Emotional balance comes from a deliberate choice to accept healthy choices and reject unhealthy choices. Nourishing your followers and rewarding them for healthy choices will breed a balanced lifestyle. Spend time with your follower and talk to them about their choices. Surround yourself with people that have positive attitudes and have time to serve others. People with giving hearts will have a tendency to be more balanced in their thinking.

CONCLUSION—BUILDING A CLASSROOM WITH EMOTIONAL FORTITUDE

Effective leadership is a result of emotional credibility. Having a strong sense of emotional balance helps followers to recognize their own need for balance. Building emotional fortitude is a process that requires that you nourish your own emotional balance by building your character and holding fast to your values. When you are sure of your values you can build a system that works even in the face of challenges.

You can aid your students with emotional balance by offering the following:

✓ **Step 1:** Tell your students to surround themselves with people that will help them build their character.

✓ **Step 2:** Create a positive atmosphere of emotional healing by acknowledging every students worth. Teach them to acknowledge one another's worth.

✓ **Step 3:** Show them that setting goals and referring to their SWOT will help them to adjust to change.

As you move through your own emotional awareness recognize the areas of strength that build others. Aid your followers by teaching the importance of emotional balance.

11

Climate Control

That is true culture which helps us to work for the social betterment of all.
~Henry Ward Beecher

Culture of the mind must be subservient to the heart.
~Mahatma Gandhi

*If we cannot end now our differences, at least we can
help make the world safe for diversity.*
~John F. Kennedy

Culture is the widening of the mind and of the spirit.
~Jawaharlal Nehru

*Preservation of one's own culture does not require
contempt or disrespect for other cultures.*
~Cesar Chavez

I am large. I contain multitudes.
~Walt Whitman

STRATEGY: HARNESS THE POWER OF DIVERSITY

AS THE WORLD TURNS

Hurricane Katrina and Tsunami were cataclysmic environmental events that affected hundreds and thousands of people and altered perhaps forever the way we look at the environment.

But hurricanes are nothing new. In the United States, the Caribbean, Asia. and other parts of the world, we plot the annual cycle of hurricanes and give them special names like Gilbert, Frederick, David and Katrina. The same goes for earthquakes, floods, avalanches and other natural disasters. They are a part of life on earth. Every class in physical geography has something to say about shifts in the earth's crust, rising or receding water levels, deforestation, and global warming.

The environment it seems is with us wherever we go. In many countries The Weather Channel caters to this interest. Elsewhere, the nightly weather which always follows the local news and sports keeps us on our toes even if we only listen with half an ear. We have heard most of it before. Precipitation, cloud formations, gusty winds, cold fronts, Doppler radar, El Niño, and global warming. As the world turns it appears that the environment is becoming more important. Yet our globe is much more than just another planet rotating in space.

The earth is made up of different weather and other zones. Hot, cold, temperate, humid, arid, arctic, monsoon, desert, rainfall, and rainforest. We know them all. The differences are part of what keeps the world turning. They help to maintain the balance or homeostasis of the globe. They also contribute to our different cultures, colors, languages, foods, and living habits.

In some ways the classroom can be viewed as a global project. Even if individual classrooms appear pretty uniform in terms of their student configuration they may still be approached as global experiments. The first point worth noting is that the sphere we call the globe has no corners. It is also dynamic. If the globe were to stop rotating even for a single second, life as we know it would cease to exist. To survive we have to keep moving.

In classroom terms this translates not just into activity but also innovation and creativity. Classrooms that operate "in the round" emphasize the importance of being part of the circle. Turning and turning we maintain our balance and by the same process are united. The mix of land, water, ice-capped mountains, desert, city and rural village together to make up our globe. The transformational classroom is a potential microcosm of the globe. And at a time when global warming seems to be on everybody's lips, the classroom can be one place where climate control can be seen to work. Climate control is really about balance and increased synergies. Ultimately, it refers to how effective we are at managing or regulating the cultural environments that are our classrooms.

THE MIRROR

Trying to make sense of who we are keeps some people awake at night while others, who presumably know who they are, simply get on with the business of life. For the majority, a name, physical description, address, religion, cultural heritage, profession, official government ID (and possibly at least one credit card) are all that are required to survive. But if these are not enough creativity steps in to fill the gap. This is where nicknames, hairstyles, hobbies, musical tastes and inscriptions on the backs of leather jackets or T-shirts come in useful.

Today virtually everything we do is organized around communities, teams and, increasingly, online social networking groups. Everything from scrabble and sports fan clubs to dating, cosmetic surgery, and global security is organized with the group in mind. We like being part of groups, they make us human. Belonging is an essential part of what it means to be human and civilized. Almost from birth we are told that too much individuality will not work, although to some extent this depends on where we happen to be born or raised. Generally speaking though the dangers of narcissism are part of what bind us together in communal associations of one sort or another. The idea of everyone doing their own thing is said to be confusing. The result of this is that we are encouraged to file away a big chunk of ourselves. The group is more important than the individual. Working together we are told is the better way. We can achieve much more than if each of worked alone. This is the argument of synergy. By coming together we enable the world to rotate more efficiently. And we are, hopefully, happier.

Is this really true? Returning to the song above, "When you look in the mirror *what do you see?*" Do we focus on the individual or the group? Some people see both. Deciding which is more important, the individual or the group, is not really helpful. The truth is we must somehow factor both into our thinking. Both are necessary.

IWE (I–We)
GROUPINDIVIDUAL (Group–Individual)
INDIVIDUALTEAM (Individual–Team)
MESOCIETY (Me–Society)

The important question is: Where should the emphasis be placed? And doesn't this depend on the circumstances? In the classroom should we focus on the individual or the group? Do transformational leaders in the classroom concentrate on the individual or the class?

In many societies laws safeguard individual rights. At the same time most people take pride in their communities, and may belong to an assortment of clubs, societies, and associations. A wide variety of institutions and organizations are built on relationships. Even the most ant-social or hermit needs others. The world is a rich mix of peoples, cultures, and beliefs. Individuals and groups then are important. Differences are important too. They make life much more complex, sometimes even complicated. Diversity makes for a very rich tapestry. Each individual strand contributes to the final tapestry. In the classroom teachers establish order and cohesiveness through collaboration. They also encourage creativity and innovation. Recognizing differences, especially cultural diversity, adds value to the learning agenda. In some places diversity has become a controversial concept. So-called political correctness has given it a bad name.

The best teachers are constantly on the lookout for resources and techniques that will build transformational classrooms. Anything that can increase the potential to learn and harness student progress is immediately seized upon. Properly understood and used diversity leverages the uniqueness that exists in society. Individuals and groups come together to celebrate both individual and group characteristics. One reinforces the other.

Diversity is not just for some or the few. It is not something relegated to an exotic parade or special cultural dance on International Day. Everyone can be a part of the diversity celebrations because diverse is what we all are.

All students should be afforded the opportunity to express themselves and share in an expanded cultural mix.

NO COOKIE CUTTERS HERE

Teachers must resist the one-size-fits-all or the cookie-cutter approach to teaching. This can be a tough call, particularly when institutional goals and statutory standards exert a powerful hold over developments within the school. Devising innovative and creative teaching methods is often easier said than done. But teachers who put something of themselves into the process are usually the ones who come out on top. How can this "personal branding" be accomplished?

Branding Tips

Put something of yourself into the teaching mix.

1. Devise fun, memorable exercises or approaches to learning. These do not have to be empty ploys to get student's attention. Use whatever natural strengths you possess. Think of props or any device that helps to make a point. Look at gimmick as meaningful motion, commotion, and emotion. You will be surprised at what a little color, pizzazz, and action can achieve (example, wearing a Superman outfit, complete with cape to communicate service and courage).

2. Reinforce learning using drama, dance, music or other artistic tools (example, delivering your history class as a Gandhi or Toussaint L'Ouverture soliloquy, concluding each class period with students dancing the conga leadership dance, or setting parts of the constitution to music and encouraging students to learn specific clauses and amendments in song or verse).

3. Biography—sharing your life story. This may be the best way to brand your teaching. What lessons can you share from your own personal experience? This can be used in most classes. Genealogy, oral history, language arts, travel, careers, science, and technology are just some of the areas where you can inject yourself into the class. Obviously, what you share should be appropriate. It helps if you think through the story in advance and write down the points you want to make and the lessons you expect students to draw.

While each of the three tips above will help to brand your class with your own distinctive signature a better and more inclusive way to do this is harnessing your students' distinctive qualities. What makes each individual unique? What can you say about Arun or Joshua that points to their distinctive qualities? While teachers often concentrate on academic or performance distinction a lot more could be achieved if we accepted that every single student was part of a unique cultural group with something distinctive to say. Coming into the classroom we would then say that every student starts off with a distinction.

If this sounds too simple, perhaps it is why we overlook it. Highlighting each student's cultural distinctiveness or uniqueness is another way of saying that each individual is valued. Students who are valued are more likely to develop positive bonds with their teachers and classmates (Figure 11.1).

Figure 11.1: Belonging and Respect

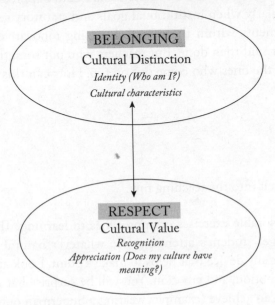

Source: Authors

Cultural distinctiveness emphasizes aspects of identity and belonging, while cultural value is about recognition and appreciation. The absence of any one of these makes it difficult for classrooms to maximize their potential. Belonging and respect cement the relationship between the student, the teacher, and the classroom (Table 11.1).

Table 11.1: Harvesting Belonging and Respect—4 Steps

Steps	Belonging (Cultural Identity)	Respect (Cultural Value)
Step 1: Develop awareness	• Learn as much as you can about different cultures from your students as well as from other sources • Avoid stereotypes • Wherever possible allow students to define themselves.	• List the values or benefits of each culture (historical, linguistic, inventions, food, personalities etc.) • Don't rank cultures • Listen (you may not be the expert)

Steps	Belonging (Cultural Identity)	Respect (Cultural Value)
	• Students can belong to several different cultures.	• Invite "cultural ambassadors" into your class (these can be relatives, persons from your local community, and other representatives)
Step 2: A voyage of discovery	• Stay current. Yesterday's cultural knowledge is not enough. Find out what's happening today. • Dig deeper. Don't just focus on the exotic. What special or interesting cultural features can you or your students uncover (example, Indian space program or Ethiopian Falasha Jews). • Build up the classroom body. Share your new discoveries with others.	• Let your class know that cultures are dynamic. Find some examples (use history, inventions, social change, urbanism, technology). • Organize cultural trips. These can be actual (museums, cultural neighborhoods, exchange visits, partnering with schools and colleges locally and overseas) or virtual using the tremendous powers now available through the Internet. • Encourage students to share three new things that they have learned (keeps them learning actively).
Step 3: Make connections	• Draw linkages between different cultures, countries, and societies. No one is an island.(example, history, religion, national holidays, international finance, manufacturing, fashion, the Internet, popular culture, Coca Cola, World War II, United Nations, etc.) • Get students to share on how their individual cultures are related. Focus on the interdependency of cultures.	• Think across disciplines. Interdisciplinary and multidisciplinary learning will help reinforce the message that culture is relevant in all contexts. Relate culture to all subjects (history, arts, science, languages, mathematics, music, engineering, social sciences, etc.) • Address your student's questions about the inherent "superiority" or "inferiority" of individual cultures honestly and factually. Talk about the value-laden meaning of the terms "superiority" and "inferiority."

(Table 11.1 Continued)

Steps	Belonging (Cultural Identity)	Respect (Cultural Value)
	• Ask students to compare and contrast their culture with others. What can they conclued from the similarities and differences?	• Get students to collaborate in drawing up an inter-cultural manifesto that states what they will do to promote cultural cooperation.
Step 4: Celebrate!	• Identify major cultural themes (holidays, language, customs etc.). Use these as a basis for learning and sharing (games, competitions, collaborative exercises, special projects, scholarship essays) • Use Banners, Flags and Emblems to represent the different cultures present in your classroom. • Form student working parties to come up with ideas for celebrating culture in the classroom.	• Values in action. Develop community partnership projects that allow you to showcase classroom cultural activities (service learning, fundraising, special gala events, parades, sports competitions, reports on exchange visits, volunteer projects). • Spread the word. Tell others about what you are doping. Share tips and resources. Invite others to your celebrations. • Go back and look at your reasons for valuing culture. Are they valid, appropriate? Do you need to change anything? Make sure that your cultural celebrations are in line with your values. Be true to yourself. The celebrations must be valuable to your students as well as to you.

Source: Authors

CONCLUSION—BUILDING DIVERSITY INTO YOUR CLASSROOM

The main lesson of this chapter is to say that teaching and learning do not occur in a cultural vacuum. Unlike the modern accouterments of popular culture which seem to be external, culture goes much deeper. Transformational teachers can help students make the connection to their authentic selves and in the process bring added value to the classroom. They do this by:

✓ **Step 1:** Addressing the strengths of each culture.
✓ **Step 2:** Highlighting key principles of mutual cooperation.
✓ **Step 3:** Encouraging positive interaction.

Promoting cooperation and positive cultural exchange prepares us not just to ride the crest of the wave but to actually calm the waters.

Social scientists tell us that society is made up of many different in-groups and out-groups. Apparently, we all belong to some groups and are excluded from others. Belonging is everything. Within the classroom, the challenge is to encourage the development of cultural in-groups without the corresponding out-groups. Sharing, ensuring that everyone has a cultural badge, and regularly emphasizing the linkages (co-dependence) between different cultures help counter the development of out-groups. Cultural belonging should be a win-win situation.

Effective win-win strategies:

- Recognizing the strengths of individual cultures.
- Understanding how the value of respect unleashes creative potential.
- Promoting effective learning through open-minded sensitivity to differences.
- Recognizing team dynamics as a tool to build cross-functional cohesiveness and interdependence.
- Building collaborative goals while recognizing differences.

The main point of this chapter has been to emphasize diversity as an important part of a progressive school culture. Like awareness and understanding, culture and diversity go hand-in-hand. The best leaders have always recognized this. Teachers and school administrators are no different. They too find in the embrace of diverse individual cultures a positive way of uniting the principle of collaboration to the need for individual self-expression. Controlling the climate is really about helping students share and care about others while at the same time believing in their own unique capabilities. No more must it be a case of one or the other. Both are possible. Indeed the classrooms of today as well as of tomorrow demand this adjustment to a new global environment in which diversity and cultural cooperation are necessary ingredients for success.

12
Conclusion

THE UBIQUITY OF VALUES

This is a book about establishing leadership success in the classroom through an intentional values-based program. While the context and many of the illustrations are drawn from the traditional classroom and academies of learning, the significance of the points made go far beyond the world of education. *10 Winning Strategies for Leaders in the Classroom* is fundamentally a book about rediscovering the power we have to rebuild, remake, re-engineer, or remodel our communities from the inside out using a variety of proven organizational techniques combined with bucketfuls of confidence, faith, creativity, and investment in honest principles. The story we have shared here—and it is a story, a narrative journey if you want—is a global one. In the same way that the lessons apply far beyond the enclosure of any single school or college, so they too have a global ring.

Crass as it may sound; children are pretty much the same everywhere. Whether we go wandering in Ankara, Turkey; Quito, Ecuador; or Mumbai, India, the struggles, needs, technologies, angst, and even the fashions are often the same. Globalization is the culprit, although this does not mean that culture has been bypassed or is no longer relevant. It is. But increasingly, the similarities are more important than the differences. Lessons in bullying or teambuilding, strategic planning or the design of hope-filled classrooms can be applied to Kigali, Rwanda and Melbourne, Australia almost as easily as these same lessons will have meaning in Glasgow, Scotland or Lahore, Pakistan. The global factor is even more obvious when we focus on values, the ingredient that allows individuals to make their true mark on the world.

Values, which social scientists link to a host of grand concepts including ethics, mores, folkways, religion, belief systems, worldview, and moral preferences are ultimately reducible to ideas concerning what it is we value or somehow regard as central to our definition of ourselves. Simply put, values are tangible expressions of the things we or our societies hold dear. It really is as simple as that, which is why values are a universal flag or emblem of belonging.

Even though disagreements over values are still the subject of conflicts between neighbors or global wars, values remain common property. Everyone has values. Conscious or unconscious, general or specific, secular or sacred, abstract or applied, developed or primitive, values are a permanent, yet dynamic feature of every society. Past, present, or future, all civilizations come bearing their flag of values.

- Freedom
- Human rights
- Human values

Are any of these really universal? That's a debate many are still having. Initially, the point is not so much *how* we define, measure, or choose to interpret particular values. Values in this sense are up for dispute. What is more significant is that almost everyone, wherever they happen to be located on the globe and whatever their culture, will have a view on these three themes. It is from this baseline or foundation of shared language and recognition that something important is at stake here that we can move on to declare the significance of one or more values over another set. This latter is usually assigned to the realm of politics or religion, occasionally both. But values are everywhere and in a true sense are the cultural axis around which the world turns. Whether you live in Tibet, Indonesia, Colombia, Alaska, Western Samoa, or Ukraine values will attend your waking, sleeping and even your dying moments. Each day *who* you are will be influenced, if not directly shaped, by the values you hold dear or choose to ignore. Unearthing or "mining" these values is a critical/important first step to understanding our relationship to both the local and global environment. Our schools, educational, and leadership agendas turn on the significance we attach to values.

What are yours?

The main theme of Chapter 2—True Grit: The Courage to Get it Right—is the importance of developing a value system. This is the bedrock of one's leadership effectiveness in the classroom and beyond. As we have already seen, values shape us and are critical when it comes to making decisions and influencing the future. The personal analysis system we describe is an important practical aid to developing your value system. Learning about your strengths, weaknesses, opportunities, and threats guides you in the right direction with deliberate action steps. The result of all this is a deeper understanding of your values which allows the leader to find the balance needed to be effective.

In Chapter 3—Rein in the Rebel: Rekindling Hope—we considered the role of the rebel. This chapter acknowledges the reality of conflict. How do leaders cope? What can they do to defuse or even capitalize on rebellion? Instead of concentrating on the tension, we suggest the importance of forgiveness. This may sound odd to some, perhaps even counterproductive. Surely, any reining in of rebels cannot be considered an act of generosity; it might even be better described as punitive. Isn't this where rewards and punishments come in? Rebels need to be punished or corrected, made to conform. This is the usual approach. While Chapter 5—Reducing the Hate—looks at some of the traditional conflict and rebellion issues, Chapter 3 begins by issuing a call to ignite forgiveness. This is the way of peace. It is also the way of understanding and transformation. Transformational leaders are committed to helping others achieve their fullest potential. Forgiveness is the strategy which we represent as offering aid or A.I.D. to others.

Affirmation
Forgiveness comes in affirming and teaching others to be able to recognize and embrace their self.

Information
Forgiveness comes in equipping "rebels" with the tools or information to challenge, fear, and resentment.

Direction
Forgiveness comes through developing a road map, teaching rebels to establish clear goals, and celebrate successes along the way.

As any teacher or leader knows defiance or rebellion aren't easily overcome. A.I.D. must therefore be seen as an unfolding strategy, a dynamic response to the shifts and challenges to rules, regulations, order, and the very existence of the system. In a climate of what may sometimes seem like an impending revolution reining in the rebel through a strategy of forgiveness opens a gateway of hope.

At the heart of our discussion of rediscovering (mining) strategies for values-based leadership is the need to face up to the consequences of our actions. Truth has consequences. While the title of chapter three may seem to suggest a choice between truth *or* consequences, the fact is truth and consequences are inextricably linked. As hard as we may to escape it, the honest truth is everything we do brings consequences for us, for others, and for the wider community. While some of these consequences may be relatively benign, others are less so. The law of unintended consequences is also at work. Who can control it? What can we do to minimize negative consequences and promote the positive? The strategy we offer again goes back to establishing the bedrock of your values.

What are my core values or truths? Why should I care?

I care because:

1. The three things that will impact your leadership most are reliability, respect, and reputation. As a leader, your credibility is affected by all three.
2. What you say will have little meaning to others if you have nothing that you can stand on as truth. People will follow leaders they can trust.
3. To be effective in leadership you must stand for something. Your values declare what you stand for. Before you can be with others, you must be honest with yourself. Before you can offer hope to others, offer hope to yourself. Before you declare truth to others, know the truth for yourself.

Put simply, our leadership reflects who we are. Truth and consequences are, therefore, part of the daily package we carry into every classroom or leadership exchange.

Do you know who you are?

REDUCING HATE

If your answer to the above question is yes, then you are ready to begin addressing the challenges of leadership. Creating a grudge-free learning environment in which hate is unwelcome sounds like a tall order; an impossible dream. At the international level, isn't the presence of hard to shift "grudges" one of the reasons why the League of Nations was founded after the First World War and a justification for the continued existence of the United Nations? At the local level, conflict seems to be written into the very fabric of the social system, and while it may not always signal something as visceral as hate everything from debating societies, Parent-Teacher Associations (PTAs), systems of justice (the courts), and the language of bargaining, arbitration, negotiation, and political parties confirms the potency of grudges. Could any of this have meaning for the sort of learning environments we want to create? Our response was yes. Children and adults learn best when they are free to learn, when the environments in which they learn are more or less free from hate and a medley of physical and social assaults. This is true whether we are speaking of learning environments in New Orleans, Chennai, or Beijing. Transformational teachers can make a difference, but how? They can do so by recognizing that:

1. Everyone is different. Every generation also brings its own grudges to the learning environment. Being aware of these differences will help prepare you to deal with the realities of hate.
2. Challenging the hatred that begins with grudges is the best form of sharing and caring.
3. Grudge keeping is counterproductive.
4. The classroom is a place of hope.
5. The lessons of the classroom spill over into our everyday lives.

The call to reduce the hate is obviously founded in a message of individual and social transformation. Learning communities in places as culturally dissimilar as Bosnia, Vietnam, or Martinique would probably have little difficulty uniting around this common theme. A grudge-free global conference anyone?

THE FOUNDATION

A grudge-free (or reduced) environment makes it that much easier to build the positive learning communities we desire. The point of Chapter 5 is to identify the importance of commitment and consistency to the development of transformational classrooms. Commitment and consistency are the foundation stones we must lay. Chapter 6—Bedrock or Quicksand—captures the importance of the materials or ingredients that go into the foundation. The strength of the foundation is directly related to the quality of its composite elements. The lessons of this chapter are:

1. Commitment and consistency are the foundation stones upon which we build our transformational classrooms.
2. How we communicate and the values we embrace influence the commitment.
3. Goal-setting communicates an intentional strategy.
4. Planning helps reduce the tensions and anxieties brought on by living in an uncertain world. Transformational leaders prepare for tomorrow, today.
5. Provide students with detailed support and feedback about goals accomplished. This communicates the importance of coaching and mentoring to the learning process.

Few leaders will willingly acknowledge that their classrooms or organizations are established on a foundation of quicksand—some clearly are. We see it in declining standards, poor performance, discipline issues, low morale, and open warfare. Laying a strong foundation is thus mission critical. The lopsided structures of today established on a foundation of shifting sands (and values) could be the buried structures of tomorrow, with a pile of social, economic, and emotional rubble—the only visible symbols of what might have been. Now is perhaps a good time to pause and enquire: How am I building? What sort of a foundation am I laying for my students or followers? How committed am I? How consistent are my efforts? Bedrock or quicksand? How would you characterize your foundations?

THE RIGHT COMMUNICATION

Getting the foundation right makes it easier to work on the other components of the building. The leadership story is really a story about relationships. Teacher–student, leader–follower, employer–employee, parent–child relationships are everywhere and are the glue that hold all of the institutions we cherish together. But we cannot speak of relationships without acknowledging the importance of communication. In many ways communication is the subtext of this book. Value mining, transformation, leadership, and learning are when we get right down to it all forms of communication, whether with self or others. We relate. We communicate. The two go together. The message of "What You Say is What You Get" is expressed through Chapter 7. But that's not true you may say. What we say isn't always what we get. If only it were. Principles of justice, fairness, and equity all seem relevant. And in many ways they are. But the logic of communication says you get out of it what you put into it. Output and input are therefore related, even if we may not always get everything we hoped for. The power of communication (narrowly defined as what you say) to influence outcomes compels us to accept a degree of responsibility and be accountable for our communication. Yes, what you say is what you get. This makes it important to say (and do) the right thing. The simple strategy we identified in Chapter 7 was linked to *transformational communication*.

Points to consider:

1. It begins with you. What you communicate to yourself is as important as what and how you communicate to others.
2. Adapted to needs. Transformational communication builds on the needs that surround us. Every day is packed with opportunities to transform others through communicating.
3. Purpose. Transformational leaders seek to understand the purpose of their life in relationship to others. In other words, transformational communication looks for deeper meaning in this relationship. There is always more to the relationship than meets the eye. What could be the deeper purpose?

That last question should keep you busy for a very long time. What could be the deeper purpose of my relationship with others? How does my communication influence or affect this purpose? The mere affirmation of a transformational purpose will invest the relationship with new meaning. Communication is now seen as being much more than words, directions, or a simple technical exchange. The power of communication offers an opportunity to influence the relationship for good or for ill. The responsibility is mine. I am accountable both to myself as well as those in my charge.

What am I affirming? Do I believe in the power of transformation?

Don't forget, what you say is what you get.

This is why the message in Chapter 8 is to "Wear it on Your Sleeve." Be clear about who you are. Speak clearly. Don't prevaricate. If you are clear about who you are, if your values identity has been clearly established—a bedrock foundation—you should have no problems telling others of exactly who you are and the things for which you stand. This is all part of being an authentic leader.

What then is the opposite of being an authentic leader? Dare we contemplate the possibilities? It could include being:

- inauthentic;
- fake;
- dishonest;
- pretender;
- poser;

- chimera;
- unreal;
- masquerade;
- lost; or/and
- confused

We suggest authentic as an altogether better proposition. What do you think? Better yet, ask others around you.

The main purpose of authentic leadership is to lead others more effectively. The clear strategy we propose is to establish your transformational worth. Does this mean transformation has tangible value? The short answer is yes. It does. There is, therefore, something for leaders to gain by investing in declaring clearly who they are and what it is they stand for. The emphasis is on clarity and transparency. The expression to "wear it on your sleeve" is a call for you to be open as well as perhaps an invitation to others to take you at your word. It's important then to get it (the message) right. How do we accomplish this?

1. By recognizing our true worth. Truth presupposes false. Most of us have a tendency to accept a definition of who we are that is built on external circumstances or factors. Accepting our true worth challenges this idea of a value fixed by external forces. The idea of intrinsic value is revolutionary. More importantly it is liberating. I am who I am. I am important. My life has meaning. This is something I can happily wear on my sleeve, and declare to the (four corners of the) world.

2. By hoping. We are constantly growing and changing. In this dynamic of change is lodged the opportunity for transformation. As is sometimes said: While there is life there is hope. This is true. So long as we live the opportunity to change, for the positive is real. This is the hope for students and teachers alike. Wear this on your sleeve. Make it public. Tell your students that they have great worth; that you believe in them. Confirm their worth publically. Reach out to those who may have lost their way. Help them recapture their worth by encouraging them to list their strengths. These public declarations mirror what become deeper private affirmations. What is publically declared through being written on the sleeve is also inscribed in the heart. I'm hopeful and with just cause.

Teaching others about their transformational worth is vital in building confidence and helping followers to grow. It is also a clear declaration of your commitment to creating a hope-filled classroom or learning environment. This is something worth advertising. Clarify your commitments, then post them where others may clearly see.

TRUST

Signaling who you are in all authenticity increases the capacity for developing/building trust. While values and communication drive relationships forward and give meaning to our efforts to establish a transformational agenda whether in our classrooms or communities, none of this is possible in the absence of trust.

Without trust you have nothing. That's another one of those broad statements that a group of Pashtun tribal elders, gathering of world leaders, or localized school meetings can readily agree with.

Trust makes all the difference. It is the difference between success and failure in the classroom. But not only in the classroom; wherever relationships are forged, wherever people come together in social exchanges, trust increases the possibilities that the relationship will be successful. In many contexts trust will outbid even love in the campaign for significance. Trust has a clear, almost predictable value whereas love can sometimes get us into trouble, assuming we understand it in the first place. Cultivate trust and your chances of classroom or leadership success increase significantly. Our central thesis is worth repeating:

Without trust you have nothing. This could be easily re-written as...

Without trust you *are* nothing.

Other important features (key points) of trust are:

1. It is a shared relationship and requires mutual understanding for it to succeed.
2. Competing agendas and motives must be removed before trust can be established.
3. Trust breeds faith.
4. Transformational leaders inspire trust by showing their students that they care.
5. Caring begets trust, which in turn begets hope and confidence, leading to transformation.

To the above we could easily add that a little trust goes a long way. However, this is something you will have to experience or prove for yourself. Trust requires no significant investments of technology or funds and can be cultivated by teachers everywhere whatever their qualification or years of experience. In the language of business, trust is a heart investment. Invested honestly and renewed at regular intervals it has the capacity to yield an incalculable return. This is good news for teachers in Japan, leaders in Arizona, and students in Goa. In fact the chorus is far more universal than that: Trust is culture blind. The next time someone asks for a suggestion to get things moving forward in your school, or community council, or organization, or leadership conference ask them about their heart investments; ask them about their investment in trust. And the next time you wonder what you can do about the challenges you face at school, work, or home, think about how much could be achieved if, starting today, you cultivated just a little more trust.

EMOTIONAL FORTITUDE

From trust we move to the heady subject of emotional fortitude. Strength of character is where the various pieces of the values jigsaw begin to come together. Emotional fortitude is where we demonstrate our ability to "go the distance." How deep are the roots of your character? We all have stories of people we knew; of people we *thought* we knew. People who one day were okay, but then, overnight it seems they suddenly changed. Who, for reasons we are still trying to fathom, became shadows of their formerly upright selves. What happened? What went wrong? Could we have been mistaken? Take a closer look. Re-examine the contours of you relationships with these individuals. Whether teacher, leader, or colleague; relive the story. How well did you really know them? Could you really speak of their emotional fortitude? What about strength of character?

True character doesn't change. You can follow it into the secret places and you will still observe no difference. This is who I am; this is who you are; this is who we are. Emotional fortitude builds character muscles. Effective leadership, which is leadership that delivers the required results and is able to sustain these results over time, demands that leaders develop emotional fortitude. Yes, it's tough. It takes time. It is the stumbling block that many leaders find difficult to overcome. It is what results in the undoing of individuals and organizations. An entire school may fail because its principal or a single teacher lacks the depth of character and is unable to go the distance without compromising. What is true for schools and businesses has implications for nation states and global relationships. With so much credibility at stake it is imperative the roots of our character run deep. Where do we begin?

Effective leadership and emotional credibility are linked. We've already said that we lead who we are. This is honest or authentic leadership. Twisted or misaligned personalities cannot lead, at least not effectively, and never for long. Sooner or later they will be found out. In the interim we all pay the price. The best leaders recognize the need to maintain balance or equilibrium. As we know, being out of balance can lead to excesses of one sort or another. Emotional fortitude requires that you nourish your own emotional balance. You do this by building your character and holding fast to your values. Like everything else, it is not quite as easy as it might first appear. Truth, honesty, and character take work to build. Emotional fortitude is therefore a lifetime's work.

A Lifetime's Work

As the work of a lifetime, emotional fortitude is also the following:

1. A discipline of the body, mind, and heart.
2. A tool for developing others; helping followers to recognize their own need for balance.
3. A blend of emotional credibility and emotional stability.

Perhaps as a reaction against the hard-nosed rationalism of science and quantitative methods, organizational managers and leaders alike have gone in search of "softer" or more humane solutions to the perceived challenges of organizational life. Schools are not immune from this redrawing of the solutions map. Of all the techniques and tools currently available to professionals today none is more powerful than the basket of emotional tools labeled as emotional intelligence or EQ (Goleman, 2002).

- Emotional fortitude
- Emotional credibility
- Emotional stability

Emotional Intelligence—EQ

Are you getting the picture? IQ matters. Quantitative methods and techniques matter. Elements of scientific management matter. But a good deal of what we hope to achieve in our classrooms—the most powerful spaces on earth—will come from other deeply human sources, relying on nothing more than a renewed awareness, understanding, and caring concern. Leaders who demonstrate authentic, emotional skill set the stage for growth in their followers. One of the key tools in helping followers adapt to the changes they encounter daily is to create an atmosphere for emotional healing.

The compartmentalization and professionalization of functions within schools has reflected developments elsewhere in society. There are now complex arrangements for deciding everything—from the selection of textbooks to holidays, discipline, school meals, and salaries. Special schools require special teachers and special education. Students with "behavioral problems" demand armies of social workers and educational psychologists with specialized skills and armfuls of certifications. And this is all necessary. Life is much more complex and our schools must adapt or suffer the consequences. However, in our headlong advance toward an uncertain technologically-driven future, can we learn anything from yesterday? We say that rethinking the meaning of emotional fortitude allows us to recast teachers and leaders as healers.

When was the last time you thought of your leader as a healer?

Diversity

Healing is probably as powerful a concept as any designed by leaders or academics. Finding ways to reinvent our classrooms and communities in such a way that they restore balance, harmony, or peace is more than a meaningless mantra. We have the power to control the climate of our classrooms and learning environments. This can be a frightening discovery for some. For others, it will be seen as a tremendous opportunity. For the opportunists who approach the urgent needs of our students with a positive spirit, there is one more tool at their disposal. In a global and increasingly undifferentiated world, this last tool removes the remaining vestiges of opposition to the classroom as a place of transformation.

These days most of us are attuned to the demands of "ecology." Whatever the depth of our views on global warming, climate change, or the depletion of the earth's resources, we are at least familiar with the wrangling among scientists, politicians, and ordinary citizens. In science, environmental studies, or social studies projects all over the world students study the mysteries of the Amazon rain forests, the Australian Great Barrier Reef, Sahara Desert, wildlife in the Arctic, and mineral deposits in the Ganges. Given the delicate balance between humans and the environment, ecology is a must for every curriculum. Climate control, the sustainability of the natural environment, human survival; these are the foremost concerns of the 21st century.

The other main locus of concern is "community." How do we develop our social communities? In the same way that ecology is the study of the relationship between humans and the natural environment, diversity is the study of human variety and exchanges. It is the study of relationships and an acknowledgment of difference. Ethnicity, national origin, skin color, height, weight, age, wealth, social status, and IQ; diversity has many forms. In the classroom, much like in our communities, diversity influences the form and process of relationships between students and teachers, leaders and followers, citizens and their neighbors. An awareness of diversity is a must for the transformational teacher. These days, even the most isolated classroom located in the Australian Outback, Scottish Orkney Islands, or the rugged hillside communities of Bolivia's Quechua Indians are somehow connected to the world. The globe or map of the world, which seems to be more or less mandatory in every school classroom or system combined with access to internet technology to bring the world into the classroom, takes the student into the world. And within many of these same classrooms, diversity has been a long established tradition. Even in places where students are superficially the same, diversity is at work in the struggle for individuality and the expression of difference.

Transformational teachers harness the power or energy of diversity to control or actually unleash a spirit of respect for difference that paves the way for incredible journeys of human discovery, collaboration, and shared understandings. Whether we turn to the ethnically diverse classrooms found in Brooklyn, Toronto, or Delhi, or explore the turning wheel of diversity in places like Bradford in England, Sudan, or border communities in America's south west where Mexican immigration is altering the pattern of cultural relations, the inescapable reality is that diversity speaks into the fundamental needs of transformational teaching.

The Power of Diversity

1. Teaching and learning do not occur in a cultural vacuum.
2. Diversity addresses the strengths of each individual, highlighting key principles of mutual cooperation, and encouraging positive interaction between cultures, personalities, and individual narratives.
3. Helps students share and care about others, while at the same time believing in their own unique capabilities.

A lot has been written on the subject of diversity by specialists in many fields. The challenge of diversity is usually seen as an "added cost" or "burden" that practitioners in the field (teachers in this case) must accommodate. We reject this negative approach and repeat what we have said throughout this book: Anything worth doing is worth doing well. In virtually every case it will also require effort and sacrifice.

Changing

Pragmatism and a transformational agenda dictate the inclusion of diversity as an active principle in the design and delivery of learning. Changed attitudes, changed perspectives, creativity, and embrace of the possible, these are the tools it will take to make the diversity principle more than a topic of heated political or social debate. It is these same attitudes, perspectives and creativity that must be worked into the mindset of the teachers, professionals, leaders, and all others committed to an agenda for positive change.

Review again the key strategies in Table 12.1:

Table 12.1:   Key Strategies

Strategy	My Commitment	Specific Steps
1. *Develop* your value system		
2. *Ignite* forgiveness		
3. *Launch* the 3 R's—reliability, respect, and reputation		
4. *Create* a grudge-free learning environment		
5. *Lay* a strong foundation		
6. *Affirm* through transformational communication		
7. *Establish* your transformational worth		
8. *Build* trust		
9. *Generate* emotional credibility		
10. *Harness* the power of diversity		

Source: Authors.

Begin working on your commitment and specific steps—*things you will do.* We can succeed if we are willing. Transformation is possible. The opportunity to take control of the most powerful space on earth and remake it as a successful, creative, hopeful, caring, and value-based community is possible. The choice is yours.

Bibliography

Aronson, E. 2000. *Nobody left to hate: teaching compassion after columbine.* New York, NY: Henry Holt Paperbacks.

Canfield, J. 2005. *The success principles.* New York, NY: Harpers Collins Publishers.

Caroselli, M. 2000. *Leadership skills for managers.* New York, NY: McGraw-Hill.

Covey, S.R. 2004. *The 7 habits of highly effective people.* New York, NY: Free Press Division of Simon & Shuster, Inc.

Cummings, T.G. and C.G. Worley. 2005. *Organization development and change.* Mason, OH: Thomson South-Western.

Daft, R.L. 2002. *The leadership experience.* Mason, OH: South-Western.

Goleman, D. 2002. *Primal leadership: learning to lead with emotional intelligence.* Boston, MA: Harvard Business School Press.

Johnson, C.E. 2001. *Meeting the ethical challenges of leadership.* Thousand Oaks, CA: Sage Publications Inc.

Jones, G.R. and J.M. George. 2003. *Contemporary Management.* New York, NY: McGraw Hill.

Kouzes, J.M. and B.Z. Posner. 2002. *Leadership Challenge.* San Francisco, CA: John Wiley and Sons, Inc.

Levine, S. 2009. *Getting to resolution: turning conflict into collaboration.* San Francisco, CA: Barrett-Koehler Publishers Inc.

Mathis, R.L. and J.H. Jackson. 2006. *Human resource management.* Mason, OH: Thomson South-Western.

Maxwell, J.C. 2003. *Ethics 101.* New York, NY: Center Street Hachette Book Group.

Muchinsky, P.M. 2003. *Psychology applied at work.* Belmont, CA: Wadsworth/Thomson Learning.

Nash, R.H. 1992. *Worldviews in conflict.* Grand Rapids, MI: Zondervan Publishing House.

Nelson, D.L. and J. Campbell. 2003. *Organizational behavior.* Mason, OH: Thomson South-Western.

Quotes.net. 2008. Hellen Keller n.d. Retrieved from http://www.quotes.net/quote/5984 on February 16, 2008.

Random House Unabridged Dictionary. 2006. *Dictionary.com Unabridged.* Retrieved from http://dictionary.reference.com/browse/grudge on August 19, 2009.

Redl, F. 1972. *When we deal with children: selected writings.* New York, NY: Free Press.

Sanders, T. I. 1998. *Strategic thinking and the new science.* New York, NY: The Free Press, A Division of Simon and Shuster Inc.

Index

About the Authors

Bʀᴀᴍᴡᴇʟʟ Oꜱᴜʟᴀ ɪꜱ Assistant Professor at School of Global Leadership and Entrepreneurship, Regent University, Virginia, USA. He is also an applied human services practitioner with a wealth of experience that cuts across the arenas of leadership education, training, community development, and consultant management.

Dr Osula holds a PhD in Sociology and is an avid student of cultural institutions, human dynamics, and popular culture. His particular approach builds on real-life situations and needs, current knowledge, a variety of theoretical and methodological "standards", and cross-cultural thinking. His teaching, research, and consulting practice is considerable, as is his international expertise—resulting from living explorations in Africa, Asia, the Caribbean, Canada, the United States, and Europe.

Dr Osula is active in a variety of leadership and other programs as a professor, consultant, trainer, and mentor. He is a frequent participant in and organizer of training workshops and professional development seminars. His interests include: leadership development, organizational diagnosis, consulting theory and practice, ethics, coaching, global leadership, cross-cultural analyses, security, and public policy.

Prior to joining the faculty at Regent University, Virginia, USA, Dr Osula served as Director of Business Development for an IT consulting firm (Cognizant Technology Solutions). He was also an adjunct faculty member at the College of Saint Elizabeth, New Jersey, and The City University of New York (College of Staten Island). He is the Editor of the *Journal of Practical Consulting* and member of the Editorial Board of the *African Journal of Marketing Management* (AJMM).

Rᴇɴᴀᴇ Iᴅᴇʙᴏᴇɴ ɪꜱ ᴀɴ educator and leadership consultant. She currently teaches and writes curriculum based on the developing principles of transformational leadership and strategic communication. She is an instructor at Judson University, Elgin, USA, and a conference speaker.